# PIKE
## ON THE FLY

Northern Pike
*Esox lucius*

Tiger Muskie
*Esox lucius x Esox masquinongy*

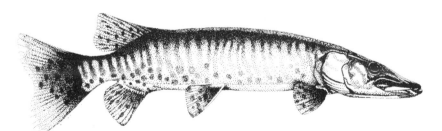

Muskellunge
*Esox masquinongy*

# PIKE
## ON THE FLY

### THE FLYFISHING GUIDE TO NORTHERNS, TIGERS, AND MUSKIES

Barry Reynolds & John Berryman

FOREWORD BY
LEFTY KREH

Johnson Books: Boulder

Cover illustration: Jay Snellgrove
Cover design: Bob Schram/Bookends

**Library of Congress Cataloging-in-Publication Data**

Reynolds, Barry.
    Pike on the fly : the flyfishing guide to northerns, tigers, and
muskies / by Barry Reynolds and John Berryman.
        p.   cm.
    Includes index.
    ISBN 1-55566-113-0
    1. Pike fishing—United States.   2. Pike Fishing—Canada.   3. Fly
fishing—United States.   4. Fly fishing—Canada.   I. Berryman,
John.   II. Title.
SH691.PGR48   1993
799.1'753—dc20                                                      93-38057
                                                                         CIP

    2   3   4   5   6   7   8   9

Printed in the United States of America by
Johnson Printing Company
1880 South 57th Court
Boulder, Colorado  80301

# CONTENTS

# FOREWORD

It was 1948 and I was casting a large streamer fly alongside some lily pads at Lake Baskatong in Canada. I'll never forget that fishing moment. Suddenly the pads swayed as something below disturbed them. Then, sweeping swiftly in behind my fly was a long, green fish that pushed a four-inch hump in the water as it pursued the fly. I had never seen a fish actually push surface water but had no time to think about it, as the big northern pike struck. Instinctively, I set the hook, and this watery demon leaped high above the surface, slicing through my fragile leader with a quick back and forth thrashing of its head. The whole scene took less than ten seconds. Yet, nearly forty-five years later, it remains fresh in my memory. Such is the impact that northern pike have on fishermen—especially those who are lucky enough to hook one on a fly. Since that time, I have landed many pike, including two muskies, with a fly rod. And while my favorite freshwater species is the smallmouth bass, I'll admit that nothing in freshwater so excites me as a big northern chasing a fly.

For some strange reason, no one has ever tackled the project of doing a book on how to flyfish for northern pike and their near-cousins, the muskie and tiger muskie. Perhaps it is well that everyone waited so long, for Barry Reynolds and John Berryman have produced what will certainly become the approved textbook on the subject. It will be very evident as you read this book that Reynolds has lived what he writes about. Only when a writer actually experiences all the joys and frustrations, under a variety of conditions, can he communicate well with the reader. This book is exceptionally well written, with text as clear as any that I've seen in a long time.

Some writers want to use a book just to display what they know, but Reynolds and Berryman share everything they can think of to help you become a better pike fisherman.

They answer all the vital questions: what is a pike, how does it act and react to its environment, where can you find pike, and how do you flyfish for pike during the various seasons. Very specific information is given on tackle and fly requirements and how to rig the leaders needed to catch these toothy critters.

If you have been frustrated when chasing pike with a fly, this book will solve many of your frustrations. If you have never flyfished for pike, do yourself a favor and read this book. It may open for you the most exciting frontier in freshwater flyfishing. Many flyfishermen will thank Barry Reynolds and John Berryman for producing one of the best how-to flyfishing books this angler has seen in a long time.

*Lefty Kreh*
*Hunt Valley, Maryland*

# PREFACE

Some years ago, I attended a flyfishing seminar conducted by a young guide named Barry Reynolds. I was going to Minnesota that summer to canoe in the Boundary Waters, and I had some vague ideas about trying to take northern pike on a fly rod. Barry, I had been told, knew more about this subject than just about anyone.

It was a seminar like many others. Barry clearly knew a lot about pike. His slide show featured the kind of appetite-whetting photos of monster fish that get any angler's blood running hot. When he showed us how to tie some of the flies he'd found to be most successful, his demonstrations were conducted slowly and carefully enough that I was confident that I'd be able to tie the giant, hairy beasts that Barry insisted would catch northerns.

And that was the rub. Like many anglers, I attend seminars regularly. Regularly I am assured by confident, tanned fishing pros that if I simply do thus-and-so, I will catch more fish or better fish or add a new dimension to my fishing. And regularly I am disappointed.

So off to Minnesota I went, fly rod in hand. I also made sure that I took a spinning rod and some huge Mepps spinners. I'm glad I took the spinning rod, because if I'd broken a tent pole I could have used it to hold my tent up. It served no other purpose during my trip. I caught a ton of northerns, all on my fly rod. I didn't catch anything very big—my biggest one may have nudged twelve pounds—but to someone who considers a three-pound trout to be a big fish, the size and strength of the northerns I caught were a revelation.

Barry's flies and, more importantly, his tactics worked very, very well indeed. When I returned home to Colorado, I looked Barry up and told him that he had single-handedly made my trip a success. And I told him that he should write a book.

"Gee," said Barry, "I'm more of a fisherman than a writer."

"Gee," I said, "it happens that I'm more of a writer than a fisherman."

And so this book was born. It is the result of hours and hours of conversations, writing, and re-writing. Barry loves to flyfish for pike, and he communicated his love for the fish, for flyfishing, and for the outdoors to me easily and gracefully.

I hope I haven't managed to lose too much of his enthusiasm in the transition from the spoken word to the written one, and I hope that I'll be able to convince you to give these wonderful fish a try.

*John Berryman*
*Aurora, Colorado*

# ACKNOWLEDGMENTS

Had it not been for the encouragement, enthusiasm, and assistance of a legion of friends, this book would probably have remained a dream. Thanking everyone would be an impossibility, but we do want to make special mention of the following people:

Our wives, Jan Berryman and Sue Reynolds, tolerated the inevitable disruption that this project involved and still believed in us. Jay Snellgrove provided the wonderful pike drawings that introduce each chapter, and Jay's brother Bryce provided photographs for the book. Together, they helped give the book its "look." Keith Pharris created the CAD illustrations, translating complex written concepts into comprehensible visual ones. Barbara Mussil of Johnson Books first saw the merit of this project and introduced us to our editor. Walt Borneman bore the formidable responsibilities of producing and marketing the book. Lefty Kreh kindly consented to write the foreword for our book. And we owe special thanks to the man who suffered through all the agonies of working with first-time writers and who was a constant source of encouragement and good ideas, our editor, Scott Roederer of Spring Creek Press.

And to those of you whom we haven't mentioned—a special thank you from the authors. You know who you are and how important you were to the preparation of this book.

# INTRODUCTION

If you're like most flyfishermen, you spend the majority of your time on the water fishing for trout or bass. When you're not pursuing one of these species, you may spend a week or two every year casting for the other. If by some chance you already flyfish for pike, you're part of a very select group.

If you're not in this group, I think you should be, for two reasons.

The first reason has to do with why you started flyfishing. You probably didn't start out as a flyfisherman. If you're like most of us, you began fishing with spinning tackle. Now, spinning tackle is much less expensive than fly tackle, and a novice spin fisherman can cast farther than an experienced flyfisherman, can work deeper waters, and can even troll. So, why *did* you become a flyfisherman?

You were most likely looking for a new challenge, an opportunity to add a new dimension to your fishing activities, or a way to somehow get closer to your quarry, to fish for it in a more intimate way. Flyfishing for pike represents exactly that kind of challenge and opportunity.

The second reason revolves around the pike itself. Look at a picture of a pike or, better yet, a mounted specimen. The flashy, jewel-box colors of trout are absent. The pike is camouflaged, ready for business. Gone are the smooth-flowing lines that enable a trout to hang effortlessly in swift waters. The pike is long, angular, and ugly. The pike personifies the word "deadly." Its eyes are hooded and seem to glare with evil (or at least hungry) intent. It proudly displays its weapons—razor-edged teeth—every time it breathes.

It looks like, acts like, and is a top-level predator. Just as you are. Flyfishing for pike is a contest between equals.

It's been many years since I caught my first pike on a fly rod, but the occasion was an important one for me, and that pike is still etched with crystalline clarity in my memory. To this day, I maintain that I was completely innocent and that I did nothing to deserve what I received.

I was minding my own business, casting what I then considered to be a huge streamer (probably something like a size 4 Olive Zonker). I was after the giant trout that live in Spinney Mountain Reservoir on the South Platte River in Colorado. It was May, the trees and fields were emerald green, and it was one of those wonderful spring days that lure anglers away from the demands of work to the banks of lakes, rivers, and streams.

I was wading along a flat, casting into about two feet of water. To tell the truth, I wasn't paying very much attention. There were better areas to fish, and as soon as some other anglers moved on, I planned to leave the flats for more productive water. Then I got a strike. Not the greedy little tug that meant a small trout had managed to sneak in front of its betters to gulp down my streamer. Not the solid belt followed by a strong pumping run that meant that I'd hooked a decent trout. The strike was faster, and it was hard.

In a heartbeat, I was looking with great alarm at my rod, which had assumed the shape of a horseshoe and seemed to be trying very hard to further transform itself into a Hula-Hoop. My line hummed as it cut a lightning-fast zigzag through the water. My poor little trout reel howled, and line disappeared from it at a rate that should have caused a backlash. Six-pound tippet suddenly seemed like a very bad idea.

Then things started to get exciting. For the next fifteen minutes, my first-ever northern pike proceeded to show me who was boss. It methodically beat the hell out of my tackle, and when it finished with the tackle, it started in on me. On four occasions, I got it within fifteen feet of me. On four occasions, it found strength for another run. Finally, it rolled, gasping, at my feet.

My little trout net was clearly not up to bagging the northern. After thinking the matter over for a moment, I grabbed the pike as though it were a snake, behind the head, and lifted it from the water. And out of the water it came. And came. And came. By the time I'd finished, I'd hoisted about ten pounds and over thirty inches of squirming, thrashing fish out of the lake.

I admired the northern for a moment, and then casually began removing my streamer from its gaping jaw, just as I would with a large trout or bass. Cleverly, the fish had saved its best shot for last. When

I grabbed the streamer, the northern tried (with complete success) to turn my hand into cube steak. All thoughts of gracefully releasing a spent fish vanished at that instant, and I simply chucked the critter back in the lake, hoping all the while that it would let me go in peace.

In all honesty, I can't claim to have released the fish. It whipped me, and as far as I'm concerned, it won its freedom fairly. With knocking knees, I made my way back to the car in search of some Band-Aids. Confused impressions of the savage strike, the speed of the fish, and its sheer aggressiveness ran through my mind. Finally, as I calmed down, I realized something else: the size of the northern I'd caught was in no way remarkable. In fact, as pike go, it was a rather ordinary specimen.

As soon as my wounds stopped bleeding, I waded back out onto the flats and resumed fishing, but this time I was fishing *for* northerns. I caught six more northerns that day. To put it another way, I caught about seventy pounds of fish. I was hooked.

That was a wild summer. I read everything I could find about fly-fishing for northerns. Unfortunately, that's not saying much; there simply isn't much out there to read. I learned as much as I could about their habits in an effort to develop strategies that would allow me to take pike consistently on fly tackle. I called our Division of Wildlife to see where I could find the fish locally. And I made mistakes—hundreds of frustrating, annoying mistakes.

I was then, and still am, a guide. During that first summer, I'd take my clients to various Colorado lakes and get them set up to catch trout. When I had a moment, and if my clients were the sort who didn't need or want my constant supervision, I'd take a moment to throw ever-larger, ever-uglier flies at long, lurking, torpedo-shaped shadows that I hoped were northerns. Sometimes they actually were northerns, and that kept me coming back for more.

As the years passed, the flies I used gradually got bigger, and the rods I used got heavier. So did the pike—lots bigger and lots heavier. By trial and error, I developed leader systems that would stand up to the razor-edged teeth and powerful jaws of an enraged northern and that would still cast reasonably well. From "huge" size 4 streamers, I moved up to size 2/0 saltwater-sized streamers and bugs, some of them over six inches long, and I threw the hairy things with nine- to ten-foot, nine-weight rods.  I was catching twenty-pound fish fairly often, and more and more regularly, the clients I guided were beginning to show interest in fishing for northerns instead of trout.

That interest became the driving force behind this book. I hope I'll be able to communicate the excitement of flyfishing for pike— a game fish every bit the equal of other species flyfishermen regularly pursue. The tactics, flies, and tackle I'll describe for you have worked for me in the giant lakes of the Far North, in rivers, in mountain reservoirs, and in ponds.

I think they'll work for you, too. Now, let's go catch a pike!

*Barry Reynolds,*
*Aurora, Colorado*

# ONE

# GETTING STARTED

**M**y first pike caught on a fly rod was an accident, as I described in the introduction, but that fish and the ten years of flyfishing for pike that followed have changed my life. I once guided only for trout, but now my guiding activities consist almost exclusively of taking clients out for northern pike or tiger muskies. In the off-season, I conduct seminars on flyfishing tactics for northern pike and teach fly-tying techniques for the patterns that I've found to take pike most consistently.

The thrill that I experienced from my first northern is still as vivid as the day it happened. Flyfishing for pike is just as exciting now, and in fact, as the fish get bigger, so does the thrill. In August of 1992, I was fortunate enough to land a fly-rod world record tiger muskie (National Fresh Water Fishing Hall of Fame, six pound leader). A world record is a once-in-a-lifetime event, but this fish was especially rewarding. You see, I knew what lake to go to, I knew where the tiger was in the lake, I knew what it was likely to hit, and I knew that I had a good chance of catching it. Ten years of experience made me confident that I could catch a record fish. Hopefully, this book will help you learn to stalk pike just as successfully and in a lot less time.

Those ten years marked some dramatic changes in all aspects of our sport, as well. Interest in flyfishing grew with unprecedented rapidity. Formerly uncrowded streams and lakes received more fishing pressure, and the crowded conditions caused, in many cases, unpleasant experiences for anglers who were used to better things.

But anglers are nothing if not innovative. Faced with crowded streams, diminishing populations of trout, and the increase of private water in many areas, wily anglers throughout America began investigating flyfishing opportunities for fish other than trout. In the course of doing so, a few fortunate anglers discovered the pike family.

Northern pike, its larger, rarer cousin the muskellunge, and the flashy hybrid tiger muskie represent the best opportunities in the lower forty-eight states for flyfishermen to catch a twenty-pound or larger fish in freshwater. And, because pike occur naturally or are stocked in about thirty-five states, the odds are good that you can land a big pike without driving very far from home.

Often, sight-fishing tactics can be used to take very large pike, making the sport even more interesting. Given appropriate water temperatures, pike can be found in shallow water, accessible to shore and wade fishermen, at many times during the year. In the spring, twenty-pound monsters will routinely cruise water that's barely deep enough to cover them. As spring changes to summer, belly boaters and boat fishermen using sinking lines find pike in the cooler depths, but when a cold front or thundershower cools the water, big pike will often move back into the shallows for a few days, providing another opportunity for wading flyfishermen to land large pike. And although the fishing is tougher, fall offers the flyfisherman some final chances to take pike in shallow water.

In some ways, fishing the shallows for pike is like bonefishing (and a lot cheaper than a trip to Christmas Island). Very often, you'll see your quarry. Sometimes, repeated casts to a cruising fish are ignored or result in a frustrating "follow," wherein a northern, like a bonefish, will trail your fly almost to your feet before it quietly drifts off. Most of the time, however, the big pike you're casting to will simply disappear. That's because the fish has accelerated from a slow cruise to thirty miles per hour in about one-and-a-half times its body length, literally charging the fly. In one instant, your fly is out of sight. In another, your tackle is in real danger.

### Why Fly Tackle?

I don't fish for pike with fly tackle because it's more sporting, although I think it does give the fish a more even chance. I don't fish for pike with fly tackle because I'm a "purist" either, although I suppose that, over the years, I've become one to some extent. Nor do I use fly tackle because I think it causes less harm to the fish, although I think that's probably the case.

The reason I fish for pike with fly tackle is because it's fun and it works. Because, over the course of ten years of fumbling and trying

Pike represent the flyfisherman's best opportunity to catch a twenty-pound or larger fish in freshwater. *B. Snellgrove.*

lots of things that didn't work, I've managed to develop techniques that consistently allow me and my clients to take large pike on fly tackle. Better tackle has helped. Longer, lighter, more powerful third-generation graphite rods make casting the jumbo flies required for pike a simpler task than it once was. New line tapers help anglers cast better than ever before and, thereby, present big flies to pike more effectively. New dyes and materials have allowed fly tiers to design effective and durable flies that will withstand the pike's teeth.

In the pages that follow, I'll teach you how to take pike reliably on fly tackle. I want to share with you the excitement of flyfishing for these strong, aggressive, "beautiful" fish.

### What We'll Cover

We'll begin with the fish, because that's what it's all about. I'll discuss the life cycle of pike and describe the differences among the three kinds of pike. In doing so, I hope to dispel some myths concerning pike. Contrary to what you may have heard, for instance, pike take a fly readily, provided that the fly is large enough to engage the interest of a predator that can eat a fish one-third its own size without difficulty and provided that you're throwing the fly where the fish are.

We'll also talk about pike habitat in chapter 2, because before you can catch pike on the fly, you must know where they can be found. If the water remains cool enough, pike can thrive in rivers, streams, lakes, and reservoirs, but the trick is in understanding where they are in those waters.

In succeeding chapters, we'll follow pike through the seasons. These chapters are really the meat of this book, the portion that discusses specific tactics you can use in spring, summer, and fall. All of these seasons present unique opportunities to the pike angler, but they also present their own special challenges.

For example, spring is the very best time to fish for pike, the time of year when pike are most accessible to the flyfisherman. But "spring" can mean different things in different places, and I'll discuss that in chapter 3. To take advantage of this prime season, you'll need to account for many confusing factors, and I'll cover them in that chapter.

Summer means warmer waters, a time when pike head for cooler, deeper water. Some flyfishermen feel that this places pike beyond their reach, but it doesn't. Cold fronts, thundershowers, and even cool evenings and mornings can even bring pike back into the shallows. Chapter 4 covers how a knowledgeable flyfisherman can continue to catch pike in summer.

Fall marks the third active time for pike. Overall, it's probably the toughest time to catch pike, but it's also a good time to catch large pike, provided you're willing to work for them. Forage fish are at their most numerous, and cooler temperatures will occasionally bring big pike back into the shallows. Like many animals, pike also

Pike can be found in the shallows in all seasons. *B. Snellgrove.*

feed heavily to help them withstand the rigors of winter. I'll give you specific tactics in chapter 5 that will make your pursuit of autumn pike productive.

Although pike are primarily a lake fish, they do also live in rivers where the current is gentle enough or where there are "lies" where they can avoid the current. Floating a river for pike can be terrific sport, so I've also included a chapter that will help you take pike from moving water.

If you're patient and willing to give the strategies and tactics I discuss in this book a try, you'll become proficient at taking pike on fly tackle. When that happens, I think you'll become a true believer, a convert to flyfishing for pike. As a true believer, you'll probably want to make a pilgrimage to mecca. For the pike flyfisherman, mecca lies to the north, in giant, cold Canadian lakes. I've spent a great deal of time in Canada, and chapter 7 will help you be successful there.

After you've caught a few pike, you may wonder what it takes to catch a real monster. Chapter 8 is devoted to special tactics that apply to the pursuit of genuine trophy fish. The final chapter on fishing for pike, chapter 9, covers strategies and tactics needed to take tiger muskies consistently. Because they're sterile and can't overpopulate, tigers are increasingly placed in waters across the country, and because they're a hybrid, they don't behave precisely the way either of their parents do.

In chapter 10 I'll discuss gear and tackle. I'll recommend the kinds of rods, reels, and other tackle you'll need for pike. You can catch pike on heavy trout gear, but as your skill improves and you become more confident in your ability to take pike, I think you'll want to get tackle that does the job better. Lines and leaders are especially important in pike fishing. Modern bug-tapers can make casting heavy flies a near-pleasant exercise, and over the years, a variety of wire and hard-mono leader designs have been developed that will stand up to pike. I'll discuss them and a lot of other gear that may be appropriate for you as a pike angler in chapter 10.

In the final chapter, I'll present some fly patterns I've found to be effective. Remember, pike flies are *big*. That makes them expensive to buy, but easy to tie. And since pike savage everything they grab, you'll need a lot of flies. The good news is that you can put your expensive dry-fly necks away. Pike flies are tied with inexpensive materials: deer hair, rabbit strips, and saddle feathers. If you have a basic selection of fly-tying tools, the only addition you're likely to need is a set of magnum jaws for your vise.

Flyfishing for pike is a comparatively new idea, so the final portion of the book consists of an appendix that should help you locate pike waters in your area.

No one can promise you trophy fish. No one has all the answers. But I believe that tactics, tackle, and flies have been developed over the years that will make your odds of being a successful flyfisherman for pike better than ever before. If you're already a fisherman, you probably have most of what is required: patience, a keen interest in your natural surroundings, a desire to learn more about the fish you cast to, and a willingness to experiment and learn new techniques if they'll make you a better fisherman. Let's start by learning as much as we can about pike.

# WATER WOLVES AND TIGERS

I hope I've convinced you that pike are worthy quarry for the fly-fisherman. Assuming that, you'll want to learn everything you can about the fish you'll be pursuing. I can't begin to tell you how important this is. Perhaps you've been fortunate enough to go fishing with a guide on one of those days when he really put you into fish. You had a ball, I'm sure, but in the back of your mind you may have thought to yourself, Heck, I could do this well if I fished every day, if I knew the water as well as the guide does.

I can't speak for other guides, but frankly I often know very little about water. I do, however, try to know as much as I can about the fish I'm after. On my trips to Canada, I often fish water I've never seen before. Although I'm generally with a local guide, usually he or she has never guided a flyfisherman before. So, I'm pretty much on my own, just like you are when you fish an unfamiliar lake or stream. Still, I manage to catch fish, because I understand pike and know where to find them.

It's not a simple task for the uninitiated. During the spawn, for example, it's not at all unusual for northern pike in big Canadian lakes to move several *miles* to spawning grounds that suit them. However, finding pike is ninety percent of the battle. When you find a pike, particularly a northern, it will be more likely to accept the first fly you present than is the finicky trout. So, the search for pike is every bit as important as matching the hatch is to the trout angler. Under the best circumstances, it's challenging. Under the worst, you could conclude that there really are no pike in a lake.

While searching for pike in a lake, for instance, you need to think a bit differently than you do in stream fishing. You won't think in terms of "lies" or how currents flow around rocks and through bends, riffles, runs, and pools, or about the emergence of a particular insect. Instead, I'll ask you to consider water temperature, approximate point in the spawn cycle, weather conditions, cover, and food sources. Instead of reading a stream, I'm going to ask you to read a fish's mind. I think you'll find it to be a challenge.

## Natural History

Pike evolved in Europe between sixty and 120 million years ago. Fossil remains tell us that ancestral pike had arrived in America by preglacial times. At least two scenarios have been proposed to explain how a freshwater fish migrated across thousands of miles of ocean.

It is known that in preglacial times there was a land bridge between Asia and North America across what is now the Bering Strait. Some researchers speculate that this bridge was lined with salt marshes or brackish-water swamps. Pike can survive in brackish water, and it may be that the ancestors of our North American pike made the journey across this land bridge by traveling through these marshes and swamps.

The other theory holds that since freshwater will float on top of saltwater, melting glaciers provided a layer of water for pike to travel in. Both of these theories may have an element of truth, for there are no pike in Newfoundland (an island a continent away from the Bering Strait) or in Nova Scotia (joined to Canada, but without a freshwater river running into it).

The muskellunge, which exists nowhere but in North America, may have evolved after pike arrived here. Fossil remains of muskies dating from the Pleistocene (less than seventy million years ago) have been found as far south as southern Oklahoma. Researchers speculate that the retreat of the glaciers in relatively modern times may have stranded the muskie in its range near the U.S.–Canada border.

Tiger muskies are a hybrid fish, a sterile cross between the northern pike and the muskellunge. Tiger muskies do occur naturally, because northerns and muskie spawning times occasionally overlap. Today, however, the vast majority of tigers you might fish for are bred in hatcheries. They have become a favorite choice for stocking as predator fish, because they can't reproduce. Fisheries managers can stock the exact number of tigers they need for predator/prey balance without fear that the tigers will take over the fishery.

But enough ancient history, where are pike found today?

**Distribution of Pike**

Northern pike are a very successful species. They live in many places in the world, generally from forty to seventy degrees north latitude. In North America, this essentially means from the Mason–Dixon line in the United States to the Arctic Circle in Canada. Muskies, on the other hand, are found only in North America. Their natural range extends from thirty-six to fifty-one degrees north latitude, or from the southern border of Tennessee to just north of the U.S.–Canada border. Very few muskies are found naturally west of the Mississippi River.

Fortunately for legions of potential pike flyfishermen, man has interfered with the natural distribution of both fish. Northerns have been stocked throughout the Plains and Rocky Mountain states. Muskies, because they can tolerate warmer water, have been stocked in areas too warm for northerns. Tigers, because they will not overpopulate, are finding favor everywhere.

As befits their worldwide distribution, northerns can adapt to wide variations in habitat. They can tolerate relatively turbid waters and low oxygen levels and are among the last fish to die off from winterkill. They can be found in small, shallow ponds, in lakes, and in rivers. However, because they aren't exceptionally good at fighting strong currents, they're seldom found in fast rivers, unless substantial cover is present. In Europe, northerns are regularly taken in brackish water, too.

Adult northerns prefer water temperatures in the mid-fifties, while younger fish will tolerate water temperatures into the low seventies. Northerns are an aggressive fish and are much easier to catch than muskies. On one occasion in Canada, I caught a northern that had one of my flies stuck in its jaw, and it is relatively common to release a northern, cast, and catch the same fish again. Because of this consistently aggressive behavior, a lake brimming with trophy-sized northerns can be fished out in just a couple of seasons by thoughtless fishermen. In heavily fished waters, a ten-pound northern is a good fish and great sport on fly tackle. In more remote waters or waters where fishermen have worked to preserve a valuable fishing resource, fish over twenty pounds can be relatively common.

As Lee Wulff said, "Game fish are too valuable to be caught only once." Because a given body of water can support only a limited number of large predator fish, a trophy northern pike fishery can be damaged in short order. A catch-and-release ethic is crucial.

The most common pike, northerns have a worldwide distribution. *B. Snellgrove.*

Muskies never reach the population densities of northerns. For this reason, they can afford to be much more choosy about what they eat. The good news is that the lower population density translates into bigger fish. Even in waters where muskies are fished heavily, fish of over thirty pounds are common. However, a strong catch-and-release ethic is still important in sustaining a trophy muskie fishery. Before going on, let's look at the differences among northerns, muskies, and tigers.

## Pike: A Description

When it's all dressed up to go out, the northern pike is properly referred to as *Esox lucius*. In more casual circles, it has many names: northern, great northern pike, 'gator, and snake, among others. Northerns have a variety of color phases, but in general their background color is dark, and their body is marked by seven to nine rows of lighter spots. The background color ranges from shades of dark green and olive through shades of brown. As is the case with most fish, the belly is lighter in color, pale cream to white. The fins are generally greenish but can show shades of red, even a pure, blood-red. The entire cheek and top half of the gill cover are scaled, and the lower jaw will show ten sensory pores. In addition, while the lower jaw of the northern has large, recurved teeth, the upper jaw has a pad of shorter, curved teeth that may remind you very much of Velcro and seems to serve a similar purpose. The current world record northern pike weighed 55 lbs., 1 oz. It was caught in Lake Grefeern, Germany, in 1986.

The scientific name for the muskellunge is *Esox musquinongy*. The name muskellunge may have come down to us from the Ojibway language: mas (ugly) kininonge (fish). Like its more common relative, the muskellunge has a plethora of nicknames: muskie, maskinonge (Canada), 'lunge, pike, blue pike, and so on. At least three subspecies are known to experts: the Great Lakes muskellunge (*Esox masquinongy masquinongy*) of the Great Lakes Basin, the Chautauqua or Ohio muskellunge (*Esox masquinongy ohioinsis*) found in Chautauqua Lake and south through the Ohio River drainage, and the northern muskellunge (*Esox masquinongy immaculatus*), which is native to Minnesota, Wisconsin, and Michigan.

In muskies, the background color is light, consisting of various shades of green, olive, brown, and silver, and the overlaying spots (if present) are dark. However, many color variants exist, including clear (pure silver), spotted, barred (almost like a tiger muskie, except that the stripes are broken), and combinations of these color schemes. Like the northern, the belly is pale, and also like the northern, the fins can range in color from shades of green through brown and even bright red. But the tips of the tail are more pointed than a northern's, and unlike the northern, long teeth are present in the upper jaw. Most significantly, only the top half of the muskie's cheek and gill covers are scaled, and the lower jaw has between twelve and twenty sensory pores.

For many years, the world record muskie was considered to be a fish caught in New York in the St. Lawrence River in 1957. It

Northern Pike
*Esox lucius*

Tiger Muskie
*Esox lucius x Esox masquinongy*

Muskellunge
*Esox masquinongy*

weighed 69 lbs., 15 oz. Recently, however, the National Fresh Water Fishing Hall of Fame and the International Game Fish Association have disallowed it due to irregularities in the weighing process and have awarded the world record title to a fish weighing 69 lbs., 11 oz. that was caught in Wisconsin in 1949.

Tiger muskies, the sterile hybrid of northerns and muskies, occur naturally where the two species live in the same waters and when spawning times overlap. Tigers are also now commonly bred in hatcheries across the country. Since they cannot overpopulate, tigers are accepted more readily by the angling public. Not a northern and not a muskie, tigers present a unique challenge to flyfishermen.

Tigers seem to exhibit more uniformity of coloration than do their northern and muskie parents. They tend to resemble the barred phase of certain muskie strains, except that the "tiger stripes" are more continuous than in muskies. As you might expect, tigers also exhibit behavioral characteristics somewhere between northerns and muskies. The world record tiger muskie was caught in Lac Vieux Desert between Wisconsin and Michigan in 1919. It weighed 51 lbs., 3 oz.

Incidentally, with northern pike and muskellunge, the male is substantially smaller than the female fish. Male northerns, for example, rarely exceed thirty inches (although they're as heavy as a female of the same length). Since there are no true male or female tigers, there are, of course, no size differences.

## Pike Feeding Habits

Years ago, outdoor writers were prone to write vicious stories about pike, claiming that their voracious appetite was the ruination of much good fishing. In truth, pike eat no more and no less than any other large predator fish. A study conducted for the Colorado Division of Wildlife by Larry Finnell in Elevenmile Reservoir between 1982 and 1987 determined that, "Reduced competition with non-game fish, as a result of pike predation, has greatly benefited the growth of salmonids."

For example, over the study's 1982–1986 period, when the stomach contents of northerns were sampled by researchers, the following rough average figures were noted:

- 7.2 percent of the stomach contents consisted of kokanee salmon
- 9 percent of the stomach contents consisted of non-game fish

- 18 percent of the stomach contents consisted of crayfish
- 25 percent of the stomach contents consisted of rainbow trout
- 36 percent of the stomach contents consisted of "miscellaneous invertebrates" (scuds, damselfly nymphs, and mayfly nymphs)
- 37 percent of the fish sampled had empty stomachs.

It should be noted that the lake surveyed has an excellent population of trophy trout; game fish were certainly present for the northerns to eat at a higher rate than they evidently did. Not a very impressive performance for the "vicious predator," is it?

However, pike do eat very large prey. Although fish make up the bulk of the pike's diet in most lakes, they will also eat virtually anything else they can swallow, including frogs, crayfish, mice, muskrats, turtles, ducklings, and according to the Bible-sworn, stone-cold-sober testimony of a guide I met in Minnesota who witnessed the act, at least one young toy poodle. It seems that the dog had joined her family as they swam from a dock at the guide's resort.

"It was pretty amazing," recalled the guide. "One second, there was this little poodle, dog-paddling around and having a ball. The next second, it was gone. Let me tell you, there were some pretty long faces around the old campfire that night."

Shortly after hatching, pike fry begin eating plankton. Once they become about an inch long, they begin preying on aquatic insects. By the time they are about two inches long, they start in on other fish, including smaller pike. This is one of the reasons why northerns and muskies rarely share the same waters.

Very young pike will eat fish very nearly their own size and can often be seen swimming about with the victim's tail protruding from their jaws. As digestion proceeds, the tail slowly disappears. Adult pike aren't nearly as greedy. They'll limit their prey to fish no more than a third or so their size, and a mere twenty-five percent of their weight. To put it another way, a twenty-pound pike will cheerfully eat a five-pound carp. In all likelihood, pike would prefer to eat round-bodied, soft-finned fish like carp or suckers (or, unfortunately, like trout). In most places, however, pike share their habitat with perch, bluegill, and bass, and pike will prey on them regularly.

Although I've been making much of the pike's ability to eat large prey, I've also caught large pike in mountain reservoirs in Colorado whose bellies were bulging with scuds and damselfly nymphs. The big message is that pike are opportunists. They will eat virtually anything, large or small, if they can. One day, I was passing the time watching a three-foot tiger lurk in ambush near a grassy bank. Suddenly, it froze and then slowly bent its body into the telltale "S" curve that means a charge is imminent. The tiger's fins began to fan the water in an agitated manner; I knew that it was going to grab something.

It was a fat crawdad, strolling along the bottom. The tiger was on the 'dad in a heartbeat. But those tearing jaws, so admirably designed for grabbing a fleeing fish, aren't the best tools for nabbing a crawdad from the bottom. The tiger pinned the crawdad to the bottom, and then paused, evidently trying to figure out what it should do next. The crawdad suffered no indecision. It thrashed its tail, dug with its legs, and squirted out from under the tiger's jaws like a squeezed watermelon seed. This comical process was repeated four more times, and each time, the crawdad made it a bit closer to the weed line. Finally, it was able zip into the weeds. The tiger nosed around in the weeds for a while, but soon returned to its original hiding place, presumably to mull over what it had learned.

Northerns, tigers, and muskies exhibit that same feeding strategy, no matter what the prey. They are sight feeders, and they usually hunt from ambush, lurking in and around cover. When it spots a potential meal, a pike slowly curves its body into an "S" shape, looking like a snake preparing to strike. Then it lunges forward, accelerating from a dead stop to thirty miles per hour in just a couple of body lengths. Once the pike has gotten its curved teeth into its victim, escape is unlikely. The crawdad was lucky.

Next, it works the prey around so it can swallow it head first. Some observers feel that this activity gives the pike an opportunity to gore the prey to kill it. This doesn't always work. I remember lifting one large pike from the water and clearly feeling its last meal squirming in its belly. In other cases, as I've mentioned, dinner simply won't fit in the cupboard, and even a larger pike will sometimes swim around with the tail of its prey protruding from its jaws.

On the face of it, the pike's rapid lunge from ambush would seem to be an unbeatable tactic. In reality, the tactic contains a fatal weakness. While the pike begins to curve its body into an "S" shape, its prey may simply wander off, swimming out of range of its lunge. Should this occur, instead of pursuing the prey, the pike will generally relax and continue to wait in ambush. Pike are sprinters, not marathon runners, and they'll avoid chasing prey if they can. As a predator, rated on a success-per-attempt basis, many observers rate

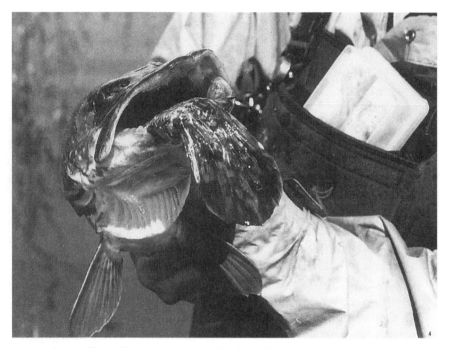

Even a large pike will swim around with the tail of its prey protruding from its jaws. *B. Snellgrove.*

the "deadly, voracious pike" a poor second to the far less fearsome-appearing bass.

Northern pike feed throughout the year and are often taken through the ice. In general, they are daylight feeders. Because of their relatively low population densities, muskies are more selective feeders and are seldom caught in the winter. Although they are also daytime feeders by preference, muskies are more easily disturbed by boats, skiers, or other things and will feed earlier or later in the day. Tigers behave more like muskies than northerns. Like many other fish, pike feed more actively on overcast days.

### The Temperature Factor

The pike's first feeding binge occurs in the spring, just before they spawn. Northerns will have begun feeding even before ice-out, while water temperature is as cold as the mid-thirties. They feed heavily as the water warms, in part to make up for the lean winter months and also to build strength for the spawn. During and immediately after spawning, feeding will slow, only to pick up again about two weeks after the spawn.

As water temperatures climb into the seventies with the approach of summer, the feeding activity of northerns will slow down. They'll move to deeper water to find cooler, more comfortable temperatures.

Muskies follow the same pattern, but they like warmer water. They begin to feed heavily only when the water temperature climbs into the forties and fifties. Muskie feeding activity seems to peak at about seventy degrees (just as the northerns are calling it quits) and tapers off if the water temperature climbs into the eighties. As you might guess, tigers will feed in higher water temperatures than northerns and cooler water temperatures than muskies.

Pike don't stop feeding when temperatures rise, but they will move to find an area of the lake that's comfortable for them. This generally means deeper, cooler water where they may be tougher to reach with fly tackle. This is particularly true in the case of larger fish, but small "hammer handles" (pike under about twenty-four inches) may stay in shallow, warm water all year long. Warm water speeds up a pike's metabolism, and smaller pike can survive and even thrive on small minnows in the shallows. The big fish, the ones we're after, must move into cooler water, because they expend more energy chasing food in warm water than the food they capture provides. In fact, in shallow lakes I often catch "summer stressed" fish, pike that may be over forty inches long and weigh less than twelve pounds.

## Growth Rates

Young pike grow extremely fast. Northerns can grow sixteen inches in their first year. As they mature, the pike's growth rate slows, and northerns over thirty inches may only add an inch or so of length per year. Northerns grow much faster in warmer waters, measuring up to thirty inches in just six years, but their life spans will be dramatically reduced. It may take twice as long for a northern to reach the same length in cool Minnesota or Canadian waters, but it will live longer and continue to grow as long as it lives.

Muskies also grow rapidly. At six years of age, a muskie is roughly twice as long as a bass or walleye of the same age. The fastest growth occurs between the ages of one and three years. Most muskies hooked by anglers are between three and six years of age, and a twenty-year-old muskie is an old fish. The world record muskie is thought to have been thirty years old.

Because muskies can tolerate warmer water, the effect of high temperatures on their life span is not as severe. If a northern can live

Deep lakes have a greater potential to produce trophy northerns. *B. Snellgrove.*

six years in a warm lake, a muskie might live twelve. But in a deep, cool lake, both fish could live to twenty years of age or older. So, look for trophy northerns in cool waters; big northerns like temperatures in the sixties. Big muskies will stand about ten more degrees. Tiger muskies, since they do not undergo the stress of spawning, grow faster than either northerns or muskies. However, there is some indication that the fast-growing tiger, even in cool waters, does not enjoy the long life span of either of its parents.

Deep lakes have a greater potential to produce trophy northerns, because the fish can find cool water that will permit them to live long enough to attain trophy size. Northerns' preferred temperature range can vary in different lakes, so use the temperatures given in the book only as a guideline. Nothing substitutes for your own research and observations.

In lakes in the northern part of the country and Canada, most of the lake may stay at suitable temperatures for pike, making the fish available to flyfishermen much of the year. Farther south, as the relatively shallow water (less than twenty feet deep) warms beyond the preferred temperature range, the fish will move into cooler depths where they may no longer be easily accessible with fly tackle. In the southernmost portion of the range of each pike, the fish cannot reproduce successfully and may remain in deep water for so much of the year that flyfishing for pike is not practical.

The pike's impressive growth figures are predicated, of course, on there being sufficient forage to feed them. Northern pike, in particular, are capable of overpopulating a lake and overfeeding on the available forage fish. This often results in a large population of stunted pike. Muskies, on the other hand, because of their relative scarcity, rarely overfeed.

In the United States and Canada, the average northern pike is about two-thirds the size of its cousin, the muskie. In Europe, northern pike approach the size of muskies. The reason for this significant difference in the sizes of North American and European fish is not known. To add more spice to the mystery, some experts believe that in the large, essentially untouched lakes of Siberia, giant northerns—bigger than the current world record *muskie*—may live, awaiting a lucky angler's fly.

### The Pike's Senses

As I've said, all pike are sight-feeders. Their eyes are highly mobile, and in aquariums captive fish can be observed actively watching potential prey. Like many fish, they also rely on their lateral line senses to help them locate prey. Pores, lined with small hairs, are scattered along the pike's body and head. Vibrations produced by fleeing bait fish stimulate the hairs, permitting the pike to locate its prey. In a pioneering series of experiments conducted many years ago, German researchers severed the optic nerves of pike and discovered that they were still able to locate and seize prey. However, when the nerves leading from the lateral line pores in the head were severed, the fish were unable to find prey.

Muskies rely on sight feeding even more than northerns do, so they do not do as well in turbid water. This may indicate that their lateral line sense is not as highly developed. Oddly, muskies have about twice as many lateral line pores in the head as do northerns.

### The Spawning Season

For the flyfisherman, spring spawning season is an important time. It's when really large pike first move into the shallows. Pike feed eagerly in the days prior to spawning. During the actual act of spawning, pike tend to be sluggish, perhaps because their minds are on other, more significant things. But they do begin to hit again soon after spawning ends. Both northerns and muskies are random spawners. They like to spawn in shallow water, over live or decaying beds of aquatic plants, but the adaptable pike often make use of what is available. I've seen northerns spawning over barren, submerged rocks in Canada.

Northerns will begin responding to the urge to spawn even before ice-out. When the water temperature reaches the low to mid-forties, northerns make their way into shallow inlets, marshes, and streams to deposit their eggs in water six inches to three feet deep. This may involve a substantial trip, and migrations of over twenty miles have been reported.

Generally, the males will arrive at the site a few days before the females. Spawning may take place over a period of several days, and during the course of the spawn, a female pike may mate with many males. The female will swim along slowly, depositing from fifty to several hundred eggs at random intervals. Her attendant males then fertilize the eggs.

The eggs of northern pike tend to sink slowly and are sticky so they adhere well to vegetation. After the eggs have been laid, the females do not feed for a while. They may leave the area to rest, returning later if water temperatures are still suitable, or they may stay in the shallows but be unresponsive to flies. Males will often remain for several more weeks, but they do not protect the eggs in any way. Naturally, the eggs become easy pickings for crawdads, aquatic insects, and small fish. Eggs that survive become an aquatic omelet hatch in about two weeks. For many years, it had been assumed that northerns spawned during daylight hours. However, recent studies conducted in Alaska suggest that northerns prefer to spawn in low light.

There are important differences in muskie spawning behavior that contribute significantly toward explaining why northerns are so much more successful as a species. First off, although muskies like to spawn in the same type of waters that northerns do, they generally spawn from two to five weeks later, when the water temperature reaches the mid-fifties. What this means is that when the muskie eggs are laid, the fry of northerns and a variety of other species have already hatched and have developed enough to find fresh muskie eggs and newly hatched fry to be a real treat. Muskies will begin to spawn at the age of three or four years, and males and females mature at the same time.

As is the case with northerns, the female muskie, trailed by her attendant males, may broadcast eggs over several hundred yards. The minimum water depth for spawning seems to be about six inches, but muskies spawn in as much as six feet of water. Like northerns, muskies are also prone to spawn in low light, and they prefer to spawn in areas where there are mucky bottoms that will shelter the eggs. And herein lies another reason why muskies have trouble competing with northerns. Muskie eggs aren't sticky. Therefore, they are more likely to fall into mud, crevasses, and the like where they don't receive sufficient oxygen. Because their eggs are sticky, northerns have better reproductive rates.

Like northerns, the male muskies will remain at the spawning site for some time after the spawn is actually over. Female muskies simply disappear. Some researchers feel that they may rest suspended in deeper water to recover from the rigors of spawning, but there is no clear proof of this.

Northerns and muskies spawn prolifically. A young twenty-two-inch female can easily lay over twenty thousand eggs. A larger fish can lay nearly two hundred thousand eggs. To put it another way, a thirty-pound female pike can lay a gallon of eggs. Since only a tiny fraction of the embryonic fish contained in the eggs will survive to adulthood, pike must lay many, many eggs.

Tiger muskies, being hybrids, do not spawn, but some observers report spawning behavior very much like that described for muskies. Opinions vary as to whether this behavior is actually the result of "false spawn" behavior or is simply because the tigers can find more food in the warming shallows. Either way, the angler wins, because the tigers, like their fertile parents, will move into the shallows where they're accessible to the flyfisherman.

## Common Misconceptions

The classic picture that springs to mind when pike are mentioned to fishermen is of a lurking, monstrous shape, hiding among the weeds in shallow water barely deep enough to cover the fish. Often, this picture is correct, but there are many exceptions to it. Northerns do like shallow water, but as they grow older, they spend more time in deeper water. Food is the driver, and in lakes where forage fish run deep, pike have been taken from depths as great as fifty feet. So, the classic picture is true only part of the time.

Another misconception about pike is that they have a favorite "lurking spot." Pike do seek out areas where they can lie in wait, but they are a cruising fish. A recent study of pike movements conducted in Canada determined that northern pike tend to remain within three hundred yards of shore, winter and summer. On a day-to-day basis in the summer, the fish moved in an area within two hundred yards of where they were the day before. So although a weed bed or a deadfall may produce pike reliably for you at many times during the year, they are not, in all likelihood, the same pike. They are cruisers that recognized a good spot and stopped to see if any prey would happen by.

Although it's true that northerns are not a schooling fish, they often do travel in close proximity to each other. If you catch one northern, cast again, because there may be more fish where the first one came from. This was made clear to me one day as John Barr and I were fishing Williams Fork Reservoir in Colorado. It was spring, and we should have been able to find fish in the shallows at the back of the bay we were fishing. Unfortunately, the pike weren't cooperating, and although we worked the shallows carefully, we hadn't moved a fish all day.

We had saved the best for last—the very end of the bay where a tiny feeder creek led into the bay. But even there we struck out. Then John moved into the creek proper. And when I say creek, I mean

Saving the best for last, the end of a bay with a small feeder creek. *B. Snellgrove.*

creek. John was fishing a piece of flowing water about five feet wide, three feet deep at most, and just over fifteen feet long. He threw one of his Barr 'Bou Face flies into the creek and instantly landed a strong twelve-pound pike.

Since I was still fishless, I felt free to sneer. "I'd like to see you do that again," I called. He did, and the second fish was bigger. If he hadn't missed the third one, I would have made him walk back to Denver, friend or not. The next day, we caught three more fish in the same spot.

## Summary

Although northerns, muskies, and tigers are similar, there are significant differences among them:

- Although color phases vary, northerns tend to be dark fish with light spots, muskies tend to be light fish with dark spots, and tigers have vivid vertical bars.

- Muskies are a "warmer" fish than northerns. They become active, spawn, feed, prefer to live, and are adversely affected by heat at temperatures roughly ten degrees warmer than northerns. Tigers, as you might guess, fall roughly in between northerns and muskies in their temperature preference.

- Because of their preference for cooler waters, northerns spawn earlier than muskies, and many infant muskies wind up as dinner for older, competing northern fry. Their eggs are sticky, so northern pike eggs have better hatch rates than do those of muskies. This means that in most cases northerns will populate lakes more heavily than do muskies.

- Northerns are more aggressive and easier to catch than muskies. Muskies are more selective and warrant the name "fish of a thousand casts." Tigers, while easier to catch than muskies, are significantly more challenging than northerns.

In the chapters that follow, we'll expand on this basic knowledge so that you'll know where to find pike and how to fish to them in each season.

# THREE

# Springtime, the Best Time

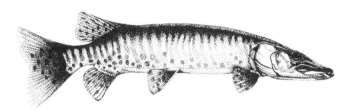

Spring is that time of the year beloved by poets, when the snow goes away, flowers begin to grow, and when, suddenly, it's time to go fishing. Unfortunately, while a definition like this one may work well for us, it doesn't mean much to a pike. Pike are very pragmatic about the seasons, and if you hope to catch pike on a fly rod, you'll have to be pragmatic too.

As far as pike are concerned, "spring" means the time of year extending from ice-out through the post-spawning season, until the waters warm enough to drive them out of the shallows. The water temperature at that point is about sixty-eight degrees for northerns and roughly five to ten degrees warmer than that for tigers and muskies. As you'll find out later in the book, lakes in the northern part of each pike's range may not warm enough to drive the fish out of the shallows. These waters, such as the great Canadian lakes, have spring fishing all season long.

As far as pike anglers are concerned, spring presents the very best opportunity to catch pike on fly tackle. It's the time of the year when all sizes and sexes of pike can be found together and when twice during a period of three to eight weeks, pike feed voraciously. It's the time of the year when pike will be present consistently in the shallows, where you can easily wade to them. More so than at any other time of the year, it's your best chance to sight-fish to hungry, aggressive pike.

Of course, the arrival of the pike's spring varies across its range. I've bumped my way through slushy ice in Manitoba to catch post-spawn northerns in July. In Colorado's cool mountain reservoirs, spring comes in early May, but our reservoirs on the plains can be fished productively weeks earlier. Keeping that in mind, let's take a close look at springtime spawning activities and what they mean to the pike fly-fisherman. As I discussed in the previous chapter, water temperature is especially critical at this time of year. I'll be discussing northerns primarily; if you're pursuing muskies, everything occurs about ten degrees "later" in the season, when the waters have warmed about ten degrees. Tigers also exhibit much of the same behavior as their fertile parents, at temperatures roughly between those of northerns and muskies.

All the temperatures I give in this book are averages. Pike adapt to the waters they live in, whether they're in Arizona or Alaska. The appendix, covering the spawning dates and temperatures across the country, shows the wide range of conditions in which pike spawn. So, if northerns generally spawn when water temperatures reach the high forties to low fifties, there are many exceptions. In Alaska, the temperature range is lower. It has to be, since some of those northern waters may not get into the fifties all year long. The range is higher in the southern states where water temperatures may never get as low as the forties. You'll have to keep track of the pike in your local waters to find the temperatures for your area.

Pike begin moving toward the shallows early in spring. *B. Snellgrove.*

*pharis*

Small males generally arrive in the shallows first, while big pre-spawn females stage at the first drop-off.

**The Spring Spawn**

As I mentioned in chapter 2, pike begin moving toward the shallows even before ice-out. In most cases, the males show up first, with the larger females coming later. When the females arrive, they'll be heavy, full of the eggs they've produced during the winter. In most cases, these big females will wait, suspended out at the first drop-off, for the water in the shallows to warm to incubation temperature.

As the temperature nears that point, the smaller males will move into the shallow spawning grounds, and these early pike can provide excellent pre-spawn sport for the angler. Spawning pike are looking for shallow, weedy areas, generally in bays. If at all possible, they'll try to combine a shallow bay with a dark, mucky, weedy bottom, and perhaps even a small feeder creek. Shallow, necked-down areas in bays and long shallow points are also good places to find spawning pike.

These shallow, quiet waters warm first, providing a good environment for pike eggs. Dark bottoms absorb the sun's heat better than sandy or rocky bottoms, so those areas will warm earlier, and muck and weeds provide shelter for adult fish and protection for their eggs. Small streams, moving limited quantities of water through sunny meadows, will also pump warm water into the pike's nursery. Large streams, on the other hand, may be running fast, moving lots of fresh snow-melt into the lake and cooling the water in a bay to the point where pike do not spawn. A perfect pike spawning ground is ten to fifteen degrees warmer than the main lake. Of course, deeper bays take longer to warm up.

If you're not familiar with the lake you'll be fishing, you should obtain a good map of the lake, such as a USGS 7.5-minute topographic map or a depth map, if available. Look for the kind of bays we've been talking about and decide how you'll get to them. Plan, if possible, to visit several bays during a day's outing. It's very likely that some of them will have better habitat and more suitable temperatures.

I've described the ideal pike spawning habitat, but pike may have to settle for what they can get. Some large Canadian lakes, for example, don't have mucky bottoms, and the pike are forced to spawn over submerged rocks. Remember, too, that spring is a time of transition. At night, the shallows cool, and the pike will head to deeper water that may be warmer at night than the shallows are. With the rising sun, the shallows will begin to warm again, and the pike head back in. If you've spotted a good bay and you strike out, don't give up. That bay can fill with pike in an hour. In Colorado, I have a "pike indicator." I'll start

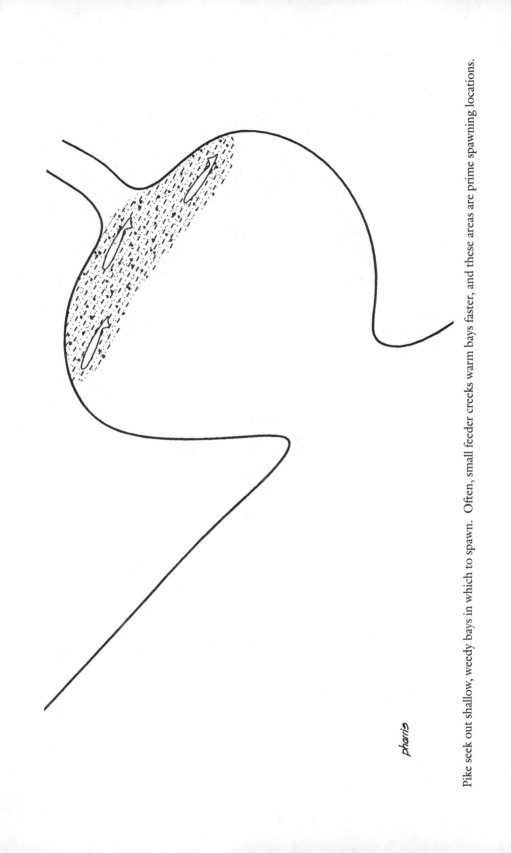

Pike seek out shallow, weedy bays in which to spawn. Often, small feeder creeks warm bays faster, and these areas are prime spawning locations.

fishing for trout early in the morning, when I know it's too cold for pike. When the trout move out, you can bet it's because big, hungry pike are moving in. Toss that six-weight in the trunk and break out your pike tackle!

I remember one cool spring morning in particular. It was when I had just begun to flyfish for pike. I was standing in calf-deep water, watching other anglers cast midges to trout. I was casting too, but instead of a graceful four-weight toothpick, I was using my big nine-weight. The main difference between what I was doing and what the other anglers were doing was that they were catching fish and I wasn't. At one point, a well-meaning fellow even took a minute to look my tackle and fly over. Kindly, he told me that I was rigged a bit heavily for trout. A real gentleman, he even gave me a nice tapered leader and a couple of midges that looked like dust particles.

I felt like a damn fool. But I am also a stubborn fool. I kept casting. The sun kept rising, and the water kept warming. Then, off to my right, I caught a glimpse of a long, ominous shadow. It was a big pike, fifteen pounds or better, beginning to move into the shallows. Fighting to control my trembling, I fired a quick cast at it. I'd rushed things; my cast was sloppy and short. To add insult to injury, I discovered that I'd been gawking at my colleagues too long. My fly had dried, and it refused to sink for a moment. Neither the short cast nor the floating fly bothered the pike at all. It charged the fly, half of its body out of the water, its jaws gaping. The fly disappeared in a flash. Finally, I did something right. I set the hook.

When a three-and-a-half foot fish is hooked in a foot of water, it has nowhere to go. The big pike's thrashing threw water everywhere, and I saw angry heads turn toward me. I suppose the other fishermen thought I was doing some noisy wading. It took me ten minutes to land that fish. By the time I held it in my hands, it had soaked me to the skin with its frantic efforts to escape. I tried to be very casual as I released it. I really wanted the other anglers to believe that I caught fish like that every day. And, because I caught six more large pike that day, in that same small bay, I think I might have convinced them that I did.

Any pike you catch at this time of the year should be returned safely to the water, so that the survival of the fishery can be assured. In fact, I never deliberately fish for pike during the spawn itself; I prefer to catch a few fish during pre-spawn, wait until after mating has occurred and the eggs have been safely laid, and then return to the

The pike's thrashing threw water everywhere. *B. Snellgrove.*

lake during the great post-spawn season. This is not just because I'm a conservationist. It happens that as the spawning actually starts, the pike begin to concentrate on mating, and fishing will slow dramatically anyway. Since not all the fish spawn at the same time and individual females don't lay their eggs immediately, spawning instead over a period of several days, the spawn can last for two to three weeks. You can expect fishing to be slow for that period.

During this time, the males will be, for lack of a better word, "frisky," and you may see them splashing around on the surface. During the time she's actively spawning, a female pike will be trailed by a group of males, all vying for her favors. Although I've never seen actual fighting between males, I have seen a group of them pay continuous attention to one female while definitely crowding each other. During the spawning act itself, male pike thrash about wildly, perhaps to scatter the eggs. This is a violent procedure and can result in damaged fins and sometimes even in injuries that kill the fish.

As is the case with most fish, the spawning act itself is exhausting. Pike need a couple of weeks to recover from their exertions. But, after that recovery period passes, a great time of the year is at hand. The spawning areas are still the warmest part of the lake, so vegetation, plankton, and aquatic insects have become active. This draws forage fish into the bays, and the now-recovered pike go on a feeding frenzy. They will stay in the bays until the water temperature rises to the point where they're driven out. For northerns, this means something like seventy degrees. In some lakes, there can be a month or so of absolutely fabulous shallow-water fishing for pike. That's why the fly-fisherman must pay attention to the spawning season; you don't want to miss even a day of the post-spawn action.

### Spring Tactics

It's a beautiful day, the wind is kicking up a light chop, and you're hitting the lake right at the start of post-spawn activities. This means that some pike will still be spawning, but others will be rested and ready for your fly. It's time to talk about how to fish for springtime pike.

I do most of my pike fishing by wading because I feel that I can give productive areas more systematic coverage that way. You may not enjoy wading or may be fishing large lakes where the ability to cover expanses of water requires a boat of some kind. That's fine, because pike aren't particularly afraid of sensibly handled boats (or anything else, for that matter). You'll do well, as long as you remember to locate areas that hold pike and fish those areas thoroughly.

In a boat, this may demand jockeying about with the trolling motor or anchoring the boat repeatedly to avoid drifting away from where the action is. Nothing prevents you from traveling to an area by boat or canoe and subsequently wading the area. By boat or on foot, let's assume you've arrived at your bay. Check it out. Is it shallow, from one to six feet deep? Look for a nice, mucky bottom with weeds and deadfall for cover. Check the water temperature. If it's early morning, and the water temperature is in the mid-fifties, it might be time to have a cup of coffee, because the post-spawn feeders will be sluggish if the temperature is much below sixty. (Remember to add five to ten degrees for tigers and muskies.)

Check the wind direction. This is important for two reasons. The surface of the water heats up first. This warmer water will be driven by the wind to the downwind side of the bay. So, if you're on the upwind side of the bay and your thermometer says it's still a little chilly for pike, the downwind side may be just enough warmer to start pike feeding. In addition, the waves, as they smack against the shore, will stir up a variety of nymphs, scuds, crawdads, and other things that will draw the attention of forage fish. If you're lucky, the motion of the waves will have created a mud line, an area of discolored water close to shore. These mud lines are the equivalent of a cafeteria for pike. Look for them and cherish them when you find them. Pike like nothing better than to cruise the edges of mud lines, darting in to nab dinner.

Some years ago, I had a great day on Spinney Mountain Reservoir. I had positioned myself on a long, shallow bar that faced a brisk spring wind. During gusts, the surface of the bar was nearly exposed. The bottom was stirred up a bit and the big pike began to stack up. I took fifteen pike in about forty-five minutes. The rest of the story is that the other two flyfishermen on the bar with me did just as well. All this action occurred in an area less than fifty feet long, and as nearly as we could determine, the other side of the bar was devoid of fish.

After checking the wind direction and before you wade in, make sure you're not going to step on a pike, because this will disappoint you and annoy the hell out of the pike. This is not as silly as it sounds. In this very active post-spawn season, large pike can be found in ridiculously shallow water, less than a foot deep. So, scan the water carefully. Good polarized sunglasses are an absolute must for this task. If you spot a fish in the shallows, cast to it from the bank. I learned this lesson the hard way. On one of my first trips to flyfish for pike, I happily hopped into the water, scanning twenty or so feet out from me in search of pike. While I don't think I actually kicked the big pike that was at my feet, I came close. There was a loud splash, but by the time I looked down, all I could see was a trail of mud heading out into deeper water and the tip of a very large tail vanishing into the depths.

Spotting pike is a skill that must be learned. Trout, since they are generally in moving water, sometimes betray their location to the angler with the movement of a fin. Pike, since they are usually in still-water, can be stationary and next to invisible. On many occasions, I've had conversations like this one with my clients.

"There, cast to the pike that's to the right of that rock."

"What pike?"

"She's a big one, hiding in the shadow of that rock. See her, just off to the right, over there?"

"You're nuts. There's no fish there."

At that point, I sneak over, tickle the pike with my rod tip, and then start working with my client on spotting pike. That ability usually evolves in stages. Stage I is when you see no pike at all and become convinced there are no pike in the water you're fishing, no matter what the state guidebooks say. If you can persevere through this stage, you've got it made. Stage II is when you see the pike after you've spooked them. If you carry ample supplies of a good antacid, you should survive this stage, as well.

Stage III occurs on one lovely day when suddenly you spot the pike before the pike spots you. Good glasses will help you reach Stage III faster, but the ability to spot pike comes mostly with practice. I hope you'll stick it out, because sight-fishing for pike is, for my money, absolutely the most fun a flyfisherman can have in freshwater.

### Getting Started

After having checked for pike near the shore, wade out so that you can make casts in all directions around you. When you cast toward shore, you should be able to place your fly in inches of water. When you cast away from the bank, you'll simply cast as far away as is comfortable for you. Don't worry about setting any records, because after you work your way along the edge of the bay, you'll come back in deeper water. You'll also be using a big rod and casting a heavy fly, and there's no point in wearing yourself out in the first hour of fishing. After all, if the weather holds, you'll be fishing until sunset.

Your initial positioning is a critical factor. In my experience, most flyfishermen who fish for pike at this time of the year cast into water that's far too deep. Make sure you cover the shallows!

Begin making your casts, working gradually around the compass. Complete the circle, move twenty or thirty feet, and repeat the process. I usually work each circle twice before moving. Move down the bay, casting as you go, systematically covering the water. When

When you cast toward shore, you should be able to place your fly in inches of water. *B. Snellgrove.*

you've traveled as far as you'd care to, wade out (or move the boat out) a bit farther and work your way back. The important thing is to leave no gaps between your first pass and your second. Of course, you'll be doing your level best to spot pike along the way. This systematic approach often drives my clients crazy. During the course of a day, I may return to the same area five or six times and take fish each time I return. If you pass an area that really looks good to you and doesn't seem to contain fish, don't give up. Remember that pike move with warming water at this time of year. Come back in an hour or so, when the water is warmer. You may find that barren area to be full of pike.

At this time of the year, there is little subtlety about pike. They're hungry, they're active, and they'll eagerly take your fly. Trout often have inactive periods during the day, but this doesn't happen with pike at this time of the year. Given appropriate water temperatures, post-spawn pike will feed from about ten in the morning until sundown. And when you find fish, stop! The odds are excellent that there are more hungry fish in the immediate area.

As you work your way down the bay, you'll probably see pike. Cast to them. In many cases, they'll hit; in others, the fish will sulk. If the pike were a big brown, you might carefully work the trout for an hour or so and finally take it when you presented a nymph just right. Not so with pike. If a spring-season pike sulks and refuses even to follow, leave it. It may have a full belly, in which case it probably won't strike. Or the water may be just a little too cold. In that case, you'll want to remember where that fellow is. Work your way past without spooking it and continue on, but on the way back, make sure you cast to it again. After the water warms, it may find your fly more appealing.

### Beating the "Follow"

The "follow" is probably one of the most frustrating parts of fishing for pike. Here's what happens; a pike will settle in a couple of feet behind your fly and trail it in, nearly to your feet, before it quietly swims off. This behavior can turn a well-mannered fisherman into a monster in the course of just a few minutes. Happily, there are things you can do to convert some, but not all, of these follows into strikes.

I can't read the mind of a following pike, but I can take a guess at what's going on. The fisherman casts and begins to retrieve his fly. The pike spots it, thinks it might be food, and decides to look it over. Here is where the problem arises. The angler has simply given the pike too much time to think about the matter. What would a six-inch sucker do if it were trailed by three feet of hungry pike? It would put on its track shoes and run! If you get lots of follows in the spring, speed up your retrieve.

You'll also learn never to assume there isn't a pike following your fly. Fishing every cast all the way in will become second nature. At least I hope it will. I wouldn't want you to learn the lesson the hard way like I did. I was fishing in Canada at the end of a long day, and I'd been casting so much it had become kind of automatic. Maybe I hadn't been paying as much attention to following fish, and I know I'd been neglecting to retrieve my fly all the way in. An old lady pike pointed that out to me.

I'd just finished a strip retrieve and began a double-hauled backcast. My Bunny Bug was pulled to the surface and made a wake as it came clear. In that instant, I saw her. Prompted by the increased speed of the fly, she had accelerated to catch it, but it was just too fast. She came to within four feet of me and stopped. She looked at me for a long moment and then turned away. She was the biggest pike I have ever seen, to this day—at least fifty inches and probably bigger.

Of course, I cast to her, but a pike that old and that big has seen enough of everything to know better. You'll only get one chance at

A pike's eyes sit far back on its head, making it difficult for the fish to see a fly close to its nose. *B. Snellgrove.*

a real giant, and I'd had mine. The potential world record rightfully ignored the fly she had just tried to take. She did teach me a lesson, though. I bring my fly all the way in, watching all the while for following pike, and I give my rod a back-and-forth motion before I start my pick up. That motion with my rod helps beat the second type of follow.

That kind of follow happens when a pike comes into view, trailing your fly. Gradually it speeds up and approaches the fly, and you prepare for the strike. Suddenly, the pike seems to lose interest and drifts back. What I think happens is this. Take a look at a picture of a pike. Notice that its eyes sit far back on its head. I suspect strongly that the pike doesn't see well close to its nose and directly in front of it and that when it moves in slowly and deliberately, it literally loses sight of the fly. Should this happen, there a couple of things you can do, and at least one thing you should never do.

First, you can quickly move the tip of your rod to either side or straight up. This will pull the fly out of its line, away from the pike's nose, where it can pick up the fly visually again. Second, you can go back after the fish. Chances are that if it was interested in the fly once, it'll be interested in it again. On your next cast, speed your retrieve. Again, your objective in so doing is to give the pike less time to think about the situation, to require it to charge the fly and strike before it loses sight of it. What you should never do is stop the fly. Remember our six-inch sucker with the track shoes? It is unnatural for a fleeing bait fish to stop; your fly shouldn't either.

There are two other tactics that can be applied to sulky pike. If you're getting follows that you can't convert to strikes, move to a smaller fly. In some cases, this can mean a hasty trimming of feathers or fur with your scissors. In others, you may actually have to drop down a size or two. Particularly when the water is still a bit cool, hesitant pike seem to like a smaller fly. Remember, although pike do eat large prey, they also routinely feed on small animals like crawdads and scuds.

The second thing you can do is change your leader system. In the chapter on tackle, I'll discuss both wire and hard-monofilament leader systems. If you happen to be using a wire system and get too many follows, switch to mono. The mono is harder for the fish to see, and I believe that the action of the fly is significantly improved. In fact, although I'll tell you how to fabricate wire leader systems, I rarely use them myself. I've found that the new hard-monofilaments are very reliable, as long as you remember to check for nicks after every, I mean *every*, fish.

## The Retrieve

In the cool of the morning, I'll usually retrieve a subsurface fly with twelve- to eighteen-inch strips, repeated slowly, about as slow as I can go. My theory is that the fish are more sluggish and won't be able to pursue a really fast fly. During the heat of the day, pike are more active, and I respond by stripping as much as three feet of line at a crack, as fast as I can. This is going to feel very awkward to a trout fisherman used to delicate little strips or figure-eight retrieves. I don't know what I can do to make you feel any better about retrieving this fast, except to reassure you that your fastest stripping will be slower than a moderate spinning reel retrieve that routinely takes pike. Don't be afraid to make that fly zip right along, and be willing to experiment with the speed of your retrieves.

There is one more kind of retrieve you may need. As I mentioned above, pike can be next to invisible. When you begin flyfishing for pike, you'll certainly spook many fish. But as you get better at spotting *Esox*, and move from being a Stage II to a Stage III pike spotter, you may suddenly discover with horror that a monster pike is sitting two feet away from you. This happens more often than you might think.

What to do? Don't back up! If you were lucky enough to avoid spooking the fish on your way in, you certainly don't want to press your luck. What I do when this happens is "noodle" the fish. (At this point flyfishing purists generally leave the room. Bear with me. You'll catch this fish and those who leave the room won't.)

I flip the fly out to one side of the fish. Often this means leader only, but don't worry, a big pike fly flips fine. Then I drag the fly around to where the fish can see it and begin to tease it. The action is very much like that used when you're teasing a kitten with a ball of yarn. Many, many times this will provoke a strike. When this happens, be ready! The entire weight of the fish will come to bear on your tackle and leader instantly, and you'll almost certainly have to feed some line. And, be ready for the fish to make a screaming run between your legs. In this event, some ballet lessons may help.

Floating flies imitate prey, such as a frog, mouse, baby muskrat, or perhaps a wounded bait fish, and they require a different style of retrieve. It is unlikely that these animals are very aware of what's going on underneath them. Rarely are they fleeing, although they may be struggling to find their way to shore. When you cast your floater into the shallows, stop. Remember, a land animal is likely to be stunned by its fall into the drink. Even an injured fish isn't particularly active. By stopping, you're giving the pike time to sneak up on its distressed victim.

Let the fly sit at least ten or fifteen seconds, maybe as long as a minute; you'll have to experiment. Then begin the popping, jerky style of retrieve typically used for bass bugs. Be ready. Very often, a pike will belt a floater at the very first sign of motion. The retrieve is not the only key to success in fishing floating flies for pike; hesitating in setting the hook is another one.

Because I'm a guide, I see lots of first-time pike flyfishermen, and I really believe that most of the problems they have catching pike on floaters are due to what I call "pike fever." The first time I went to Canada, I suffered from it greatly. I'd cast a floating fly into the shallows, and in an instant I'd see as many as five wakes shooting for my fly. Now, a big pike can easily push four or five inches of water in front of her when she's in a hurry, and the sight of five wakes of this size making for your fly at thirty miles an hour will turn your knees to rubber. In seconds, I knew I'd be involved in a terrific fight; then, right where my fly was, the water would explode in foam. I'd set the hook, only to see my fly come sailing back in my face. It took me a while to learn my lesson.

Although a pike will move at a high rate of speed to get your fly, it will really turn on the horses when it's about to nail it. That was the explosion I was seeing. It's sort of a false strike. Now when those wakes start coming toward my fly, I mumble idiotically, "Wait for it, wait for it, wait for it." And how do I know for sure the fish has the fly? Don't worry, pike are pretty good about letting you know.

## Fishing Reservoirs

Pike are a hardy, flashy fish, and they do well in all sorts of water. For these reasons, they are often planted in municipal reservoirs, and fine fishing can result. My world record tiger came from a reservoir smack in the middle of a Denver suburb, and it isn't the largest tiger to come from that water by a long shot!

Pike will hold, spawn, and hunt in reservoirs the same way they do in natural lakes. There is, however, a small problem. Reservoirs often fluctuate many feet, subject to the demands of water users. For the pike fisherman, this situation can be the ruination of good fishing, especially during the prime spring season. Imagine scouting out the likely spawning areas and returning to the lake when the big ones should be hanging around in the shallows, only to find that there are no shallows because the reservoir has been lowered.

That lovely weedy, mucky bottom is now a drying mudflat, and you're looking at a hundred feet of featureless land between you and the new water line. Has your spring fishing been ruined? Unfortunately, sometimes it really has been ruined. If the change in the environment has been too drastic for the pike, they will either refuse to spawn or the spawn will take place wherever and however they can get it done. More often than not, however, the pike's adaptability will save you.

Look at the old water line. In that mess of drying mud lived the grasses and weeds that suited the pike's spawning needs. If the slope of the flats is quite gentle, these plants might extend a hundred feet from shore; if the slope is more severe, they might stop within ten feet of the old shoreline. Clearly, these plants prefer warm water and bright sunlight. Now, look out toward the new water line. Often, you'll notice that the shallow-water plants stop growing and that there is a line of comparatively barren sand.

Hop into your waders and stroll out along that barren area. Many times you will come upon a second line of submerged vegetation. Often, the line is located at the first drop, where the flats suddenly drop off into deeper water. These are different plants than the ones that live near shore. They like deeper water and can make do with less sun. But, with the drawdown of the reservoir, they are now in shallow water, and they form a second spawning area for pike. Cast and be happy!

Another situation you may find at a reservoir is exactly the opposite of the low-water scenario I've described above. High water conditions will often occur in the spring as reservoirs are filled with snow melt or rain. The spawning area you scouted out a couple of weeks ago may now be under several feet of water, and the water may cover the grass and fields surrounding the lake. You stand on the "new" shore, thoroughly disgusted. Now where are you supposed to look for the pike?

Right in front of you would be a good starting point. Remember that in the spring, pike will seek out shallow, warm water with plenty of vegetation that will cover their eggs. Now, you may know that flooded alfalfa has nothing in common with water plants, but the pike don't. The newly flooded vegetation also provides a source of terrestrials, such as ants, worms, and caterpillars. They're a feast for small fish, which in turn become a feast for pike. So, in times of high water, fish the flooded areas.

I grant you, at times fishing these flooded areas can be a nightmare. Once when I was filming a television show in Canada, the host of the show and I fished what was essentially a flooded thicket. Backcasts were horrible; you simply couldn't keep your line out of the trees and bushes. Forward casts were nearly as tough. So we waded around among the branches and thorns, essentially dapping with our nine-weight rods.

With only a few feet of line out, things happen very fast. The pike would hit hard and then dash for cover. There was literally no slack in the line, and we couldn't feed the fish much line because of the cover. My partner and I fought panting, grunting tug-of-war contests with angry, splashing fish. Sometimes we won, and we laughed like children as we held our latest conquest up for the other to see. Other times the pike won, and we still laughed. But if we hadn't been nailing fish of twenty pounds and more every ten minutes or so, the whole affair could have been discouraging.

## Cold Fronts

During the spring, the water temperature may be barely warm enough for pike. It won't take much of a drop in water temperature

At times, fishing the flooded areas can be a nightmare. *B. Snellgrove.*

to convince them to move back into deeper water, and a cold front can do just that.

As a cold front moves in, the pike will often become more aggressive, as if they can sense the onset of cooler temperatures (and perhaps they can). When the front arrives and if it is strong enough to cool the water a few degrees, the pike will retreat into deeper water. This is not as fatal as it sounds. It's still spring, so the pike will retreat the minimum amount necessary to find a suitable temperature. This translates to a move to water as little as two or three feet deeper or as much as ten feet deeper.

The pike also slow down. If you can still reach them with fly tackle, it's time to slow your retrieve and perhaps change to smaller flies. When the front moves out, the water won't warm instantly. It will warm over a period of days, and as it warms, the pike will gradually return to the shallows.

**Flies for Spring**

With all this talk about how to handle the fly, you've no doubt been wondering what flies I use at this time of year. If you're a trout fisherman, you'll be pleased, or perhaps appalled, to learn that this is not as important as it is when fishing for trout. Trout, as you know, can exhibit selective feeding behavior. At times, if you don't have the right fly in your vest, you might as well go home and watch the ball game.

Pike are also selective, in the sense that if they can't swallow it they won't eat it, although they may try to. Pike flies are therefore attractors. I'll discuss specific fly patterns in chapter 11, but in general, pike flies are large and very durable. In my experience, it's not always necessary to find the "right" fly, although it is necessary to find a fly that they can see and one that will handle specific fishing demands.

In the spring, a couple of my favorites are Bunny Bugs and Deceivers. If you prefer to buy your flies, Umpqua's Barr 'Bou Face is a fine bunny-type fly. Many brightly colored tarpon flies also work very well for pike. These are all streamers, and although they're effective, they can be a real pain in the neck to use if the pike are holding in very shallow water. For those conditions I use floating flies. Big clipped-hair bass bugs and divers work well. Umpqua's Swimming Baitfish has produced well for me in these conditions, also. Effective weed guards are absolutely essential on all pike flies, floating or sinking.

When it comes to colors, a general rule is the more visible the fly the better. If I'm fishing in really clear water, my first choices for spring pike are white and black. In waters that are discolored, I've found that yellows, oranges, and shades of chartreuse are more effective. Also, don't neglect "two-tones." On a recent trip to Minnesota, chartreuse/orange Bunny Bugs were the clear favorite of the pike. Black/white combinations can also be deadly "two-tones."

The best way to be successful during the spring is to make sure you spend as much time on the water as you can. The pike are significantly more active than they are at any other time of the year, and best of all, they tend to stay where the flyfisherman can get to them. All good things must come to an end, however. Gradually, the water will warm, spring will inevitably give way to summer, and pike feeding patterns will change. The big pike begin to disappear from reliable, productive haunts. Summer has arrived, and with summer come new challenges for the pike angler.

# FOUR

# SUMMER, RETURN TO NORMALCY

S ummertime. And the livin', the song insists, is easy. It all sounds
great in the song, especially the part about the fish jumpin', but
I'm afraid that it just isn't true for those who flyfish for pike. During
the spring, pike anglers take advantage of a special situation: the pre-
and post-spawn when pike are hungry and aggressive and are found
in shallow water. But as the big pike start to leave the warming shallows, you'll have to learn to fish for "normal" pike, fish that are living, hunting, and eating as they do most of the year.

Like spring pike fishing, "summer" means different things in different places. August may be a slow time for northerns in most of the
country, but it can be a great time to catch them in the Far North or
in mountain reservoirs. Both tigers and muskies tolerate warmer
water, and summer is a good time to pursue them. They'll remain in
the shallows longer than northerns will. On my home waters, for
instance, July and August signal fine tiger fishing.

While summer is admittedly not as productive as spring, the per-
sistent angler can still take many pike, as long as he changes his tactics and where he fishes. Like the fish you're pursuing, you'll have to
become a hunter and learn to seek pike out in their new summer
haunts. To do that successfully, the first thing you'll need to know is
what summer means to the pike.

In the pike's environment, summer is the time when the waters
warm to a stable temperature, maybe something on the order of sixty-
eight degrees. The shallows become warmer than this, of course. Not
only are the shallows too warm for pike, but the warmer temperatures
also drive forage fish into cooler water. So the pike leave the shallows

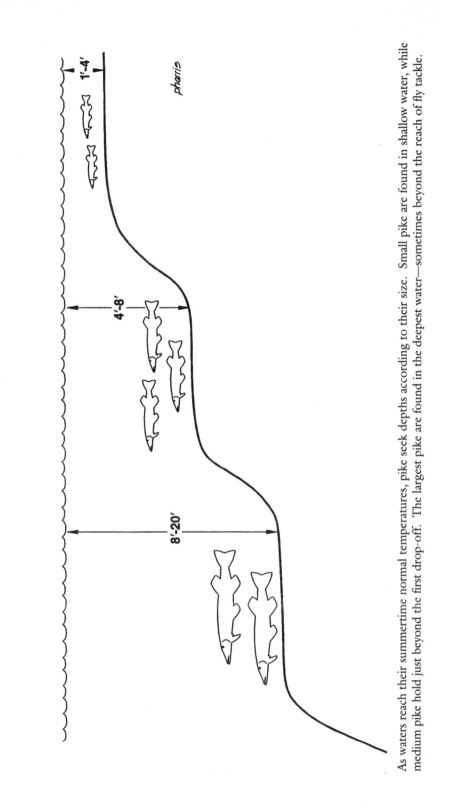

As waters reach their summertime normal temperatures, pike seek depths according to their size. Small pike are found in shallow water, while medium pike hold just beyond the first drop-off. The largest pike are found in the deepest water—sometimes beyond the reach of fly tackle.

for two reasons, "personal preference" and because their food sources are also moving into deeper water.

The personal preference part of this means different things to different sizes of pike. Smaller pike of one to four pounds, for instance, can often be found in shallow waters all year. They are, for all intents and purposes, a warm water fish. Medium-sized pike of five to eight pounds are essentially cool water fish and can be found in intermediate depths, four to eight feet, while large pike are almost a cold water fish and will be found in the deepest water.

There are differences between the species, too. Bearing in mind the differences in water temperatures preferred by tigers and muskies, these fish make exactly the same kinds of moves into deeper water that northerns do. The tigers do so at temperatures roughly five degrees higher than northerns, and the muskies do so at temperatures about ten degrees warmer. Another way of looking at this situation is to say that in the summer northerns will generally be found in water five to eight feet deeper than tigers and muskies. Since flyfishermen cannot efficiently fish really deep water, this difference can be crucial.

So, the pike will tell you when summer has arrived. Over a period of days, the size of the fish you catch in the shallows will begin to diminish. That, and the rising temperatures, will be your signal to begin using summer tactics.

Now, all of this sounds fine on paper, but it isn't as cut-and-dried as the preceding paragraphs would suggest. First, the warming pattern I've described above depends on a variety of factors, including the depth of the lake, the type of bottom, the weather, and the location of the lake. Lakes in the northern United States and Canada, for example, may stay cool enough throughout the summer to permit pike to remain in shallow water. So, once again, there's no substitute for doing your homework. On your home lakes, this means spending time on the water and making a careful study of what is going on.

It will also mean paying attention to the weather. In lakes that are nearly cool enough for pike to remain in the shallows, several days of rain or a sharp cold front will often bring them back. Typically this return to the shallows will only last a few days (and sometimes only a few hours), because the water will warm up again.

### Finding the Fish

In the spring, we were looking for long, shallow bays that warm quickly. Now, we're looking for areas that offer between six and fifteen feet of water, enough shelter for forage fish, and areas where a pike digesting its meal can hide. Often, this will again mean bays, points adjacent to bays, and saddles between islands or between the shore and an island, especially if the first drop-off is steep enough to offer the fish some shelter. It can also mean relatively steep banks, where the pike can find shelter in deep water under overhanging trees and around rocks.

Minnows and other small fish are, of course, another thing to keep an eye out for. I'm not talking about fry. I mean minnows, schools of fat two- to six-inch fish. The pike may not be eating the two-inch fish, but the six-inch minnows are, and the pike will eat the bigger fish happily. When you find the minnows, ask yourself the next logical question: where is the nearest shelter from which a pike could cruise for dinner?

Think of pike the way you think of large, land-dwelling predators, such as lions. Both are near the top of their predator pyramids. If they can, both will eat heavily. After they feed, both may rest for several hours and even days, digesting their meals. This feeding behavior provides the key to finding pike. Like the lion that trails herds of food animals on the African veldt, the pike wants to be close to a source of food. And like the lion, after the pike eats, it will want to find a secluded spot where it can digest its dinner in peace.

There is a related pike behavior that I should mention in order to save you some confusion and frustration. Unlike the lion, the pike is a cold-blooded animal. When the lion eats an antelope, its rapid mammalian metabolism will manage digestion quickly. Not so with the pike. A pike may sometimes return to the warm shallows after it has eaten and literally bask in the sun. On other occasions pike float, even over deep waters, with just a fraction of an inch of water covering the fish. Apparently, this serves to speed up the fish's metabolism and permits it to digest supper more efficiently. Although all pike can be sunbathers, I've observed this behavior most often in tigers and muskies.

Fishing for these sunbathing fish is very frustrating. You'll see a large pike, holding in the shallows, just as the fish did during the spawn, or lolling about close to the surface. You'll cast to the fish, only to have your every offering refused. You can see why—the fish is likely to be full of food.

So, if a pike is not actively hunting, it's probably digesting its dinner and will not be especially interested in your fly, but don't for a moment believe that I pass big fish by. When I see a big pike, I cast

Summer means fishing in deeper water. *B. Snellgrove.*

to it, no matter where it may be. After all, there's always a chance that the fish is nearly finished with dinner or that I will succeed in irritating it and that it may belt a fly. But in the summer in the shallows, if a pike doesn't show some interest in my fly after a cast or two, I move on to greener pastures.

Those greener pastures are the areas I've described where the fish finds what it needs: a place to hide, a place to find food, and suitable water temperatures. In many lakes, this translates to the first drop-off, an area of between six and fifteen feet of water along a weed line. The vegetation provides food and shelter for forage fish and cover for a hungry pike. If available, pike will seek out fallen trees, brush piles, and nooks and crannies in rocky bottoms where they can rest after a meal.

In many cases, if the bottom falls off fairly abruptly, this may be very close to the shallows where the pike spawned, perhaps just another twenty feet or so farther out into the lake. In others, if the bottom falls off gradually, you may be fishing several hundred feet away from the spawning areas.

You'll remember that I said many anglers have trouble in the spring because they fish in too much water. Summer marks the time that you want to begin fishing exactly that sort of "too much" water, six to perhaps as much as twenty feet deep. One of my favorite mountain lakes has a substantial amount of deadfall around the shore, the tips of the downed trees extending into about fifteen feet of water. It's not at all unusual to see very large pike hiding among the branches. Sometimes they will be literally surrounded by bait fish, but casting to these fellows is often a waste of time. They've already had dinner. If you come back to those same trees and see pike slowly cruising around and if the bait fish seem to be skittish, this is a good indication that someone is hungry and is hunting for the next meal.

I should tell you here of a judgment call I make during the summer. Pike can, and often do, hunt much deeper than twenty feet. In really warm, deep lakes, they will regularly feed in as much as fifty feet of water. As far as I'm concerned, when the pike are this deep, it's time to go trout fishing or go back into the shallows after bass. If you have a pike river nearby, summertime is an excellent time to go after them there.

There is one other important difference between spring and summer fishing for pike. During the spring spawn, pike often feed during all of the daylight hours. They're usually hungry, and they're very active. As summer comes and the number of forage fish increases, they need to feed only to sustain themselves, and mornings and evenings can be the best times for flyfishing for pike. Because pike are predominantly sight feeders, full darkness is not the best time to fish, but if you can see well enough to fish, odds are the pike can see well enough to hunt.

You should also be on the lookout for another summer holding area for pike. Many lakes receive some of their water from underwater springs, and the water around those springs will remain cold enough to support pike all year. In the case of manmade lakes and reservoirs, the locations of springs are often marked on maps. If you're fishing natural lakes or if springs are not marked on your map, keep an eye out for one of two clues. Your first clue will be an abrupt, local change in the character of the bottom vegetation. Sometimes the cooler water around the spring will support aquatic plants that are quite different from those that live in the surrounding warmer water. A second clue will be the total absence of vegetation in a very small area. This occurs because the spring flows heavily enough to prevent plants from taking root. Regardless of how you locate a spring, the area of cool water is likely to be quite small, and if pike are holding around the spring, they're likely to be close to the source of the cool water.

**Summer Pike Tactics**

Fishing deeper water will require a change of techniques, of course. At this time of year, it may be difficult to wade for pike. Now is the time to pull your canoe down from the rafters, inflate the belly boat, or fish from larger boats. I prefer to fish from a canoe or boat. Float tubes are great fun, but there's a disadvantage when using them for pike. Pike are big and they are strong. To complicate matters, if you upgrade to pike gear, your rod will be at least nine feet long. This combination means that it's tough to get a big pike close enough to a belly boat to grab. A belly boater may have to play a fish out more completely, which increases mortality. If you can solve this problem, however, belly boats are an economical, portable, easy-to-store alternative to canoes and boats.

The thing to remember is that just because the fish are in deeper water doesn't mean that pike won't take a shallow fly. If they can see your fly, they will charge it aggressively, even if it's on the top of the water. They may be living in cooler, deeper water, but they will take a meal where they can find it.

If you're searching for likely pike water and it's early in the summer, I recommend returning to those same bays you fished during the spawn. Head out from shore until you locate the first weed line. As the pike move into deeper water, this is likely to be the first place they'll set up housekeeping. In the preceding chapter, I emphasized covering the shallow spawning areas thoroughly. In the summer, you should instead cover more water. The pike won't be bunched-up in the shallows the way they were in the spring. The fish you're after are actively hunting, cruising fish. Therefore, you should work the targeted areas methodically, but you should keep moving.

**Working the Water Column**

In summer you need to work a larger column of water. Unless you're lucky, you won't be able to see the schools of bait fish that the pike are trailing, so you'll want to work from the surface right down into the weeds. If you've got a depth finder, now is the time to put it to work. If you don't, careful map work and soundings with your anchor should help you find the right depths.

To work a column of water, I use a setup that might appear strange. I carry floating, sink-tip, and full-sink lines during the summer, but I usually start fishing with a full-sink line and a floating diver-type fly. This kind of rig allows me to work from the water's surface right down to the bottom in many areas I fish.

Now is the time to pull your canoe down from the rafters, inflate the belly boat, or fish from larger boats. *B. Snellgrove.*

The ability to fish different levels is the key to successful summertime pike fishing. If the fish are in six or eight feet of water, there's a good chance they'll take a floating fly. In this event, you can switch back to a floating line. In deeper water or if the bait fish are holding tight to weedy cover, your chances of bringing a pike to the surface go down dramatically. In this event, you want the ability to put the fly where the fish are feeding. When you strip in your floating diver, the full-sink line will haul the diver down deep. I can easily get a diver down to six or eight feet with this kind of setup.

My usual procedure is to cast and allow the belly of the full-sink line to sink to the depth where I want the fly to travel. While I'm waiting, the diver functions as a floater in case there are pike watching the surface. Then I make several fast three-foot strips. The diver is pulled down deep. When I pause between strips, the diver will begin floating back to the surface, wiggling seductively. Because I'm prospecting for fish, I vary my retrieves. Sometimes I'll wait for half a minute or so, which lets the diver float up a couple of feet. On other retrieves, I'll wait as long as several minutes, which may let the diver return all the way to the surface.

When the water I'm prospecting is over eight feet deep, I use a longer leader, and I again fish with a diver. This is a time for long casts. After casting, I wait until the line has had a chance to sink. The belly in the line will actually pull the floating diver back toward me. Then I begin making monster strips again. Because the line is at or near the bottom, the diver can be pulled into substantially deep water and again be allowed to float back up to the surface, permitting me to work an even larger column of water.

This can be a really slow procedure, and there are two common mistakes that anglers make. The first mistake is not to permit the line to sink deeply enough. If you're not accustomed to sinking lines, you should cast and watch the sink rate. Determine how long it takes the line to sink three feet or so. Then, when you cast, count down your line, remembering that the more line you have out, the more drag there is from the water and the slower it will sink. The second common mistake is to strip too frequently. This keeps the diver very deep, and you miss fish that are working shallower water.

The diver won't surface if it has been taken by a pike, of course. When the pike hits the fly during the strip, all is well, because you'll feel the fish immediately. But often the pike will grab the fly when it's on the way back to the surface. With the line relatively slack, feeling the strike will be difficult, at best. If you're lucky, you'll see the line move when you're not providing any input. Strike! If you're not so lucky, you won't feel the fish until you make that next monster strip. Therefore, every time you strip line, be prepared for a fish.

For reasons best known to pike, they don't spit a fly out right away. Especially with flies tied with soft, natural-feeling materials, a pike may take a fly and wait patiently for over a minute for you to set the hook. Once it feels the iron, all bets are off. Casually stripping in line and not being ready for a pike on the other end is the best way I know to lose a summer pike.

After you take a fish or two, it's time to decide how you'll continue to fish. If the fish are hitting in deeper water, I switch to a Bunny Bug or a Deceiver. If the pike are taking at or near the surface, I switch to a floating line to keep the diver on top.

## Fishing Weed Lines

In summer, I often "go visiting" in a lake. I check out downed trees and other areas where I know pike like to hold. When I find them, I make a couple of casts, but if I get no response, I move on.

Like a burglar, I'm really looking for empty houses. When the pike aren't home, they're hunting, and those are the fish I'm after. I make a beeline to the nearest weed line and begin casting.

A couple of years ago, I spent some time on Basswood Lake in the Boundary Waters Canoe Area in northern Minnesota. My host, John Swenson of Ely-based Timber Trail Lodge and Outfitters, was intrigued enough by the thought of catching pike on a fly rod to point me toward one of his favorite bays. When I arrived after a long paddle, I discovered that no one was home. The bay looked like a naturally good area, with irregular, grassy shallows, and plenty of food in the form of minnows and frogs, but I couldn't buy a fish.

Then a fortunate gust of wind blew my canoe out from shore. That was all it took. The pike were out in deeper water foraging for bigger prey at the first weed line. They seemed to find my Bunny Bug an acceptable alternative. I caught about fifteen pike that day and four bass as a bonus. I also discovered that a sixteen-pound pike can tow a canoe just fine, thank you.

If the pike are holding in water shallow enough to cover with fly tackle, the odds are good that they will be in or around weed lines. Your fly should move through the vegetation, which is why all subsurface pike flies should have weed guards. To fish weed lines, I start outside the weeds and cast into and through them and then work my way toward shore. Sometimes cruising pike will frighten forage fish into the shallows and then pursue them into areas that are warmer and shallower than those they would usually frequent at this time of year. When this happens, there will often be several pike taking advantage of the bonanza. I don't think pike actually herd prey the way stripers do, but I do think that they will gang up on schools of fish that are vulnerable.

### Differences Among Species

In the rare lake that has all three pike species, it's possible to go to a spawning bay in early spring, set up shop for northerns, and continue fishing as the season progresses for the tigers and muskies that move in as the northerns move out. But in the summer, when the lake has essentially stabilized, all three fish will locate where the general temperatures suit them best.

In Colorado, for example, by July 1st I've generally stopped fishing for northerns. In my favorite lakes, they've moved into water that is deep enough that it's no fun to fish with fly tackle. This certainly

In summer, pike prefer larger prey, such as whitefish, and your flies must be larger. *B. Snellgrove.*

doesn't mean that my pike angling is finished. July and August are my best months for tigers. They can easily stand five or ten more degrees than northerns can, and this usually puts them in water that is just shallow enough that I can fish for them very effectively.

In warm lakes, the northerns may be so deep that you'll never have a chance to find out where they are. There are some indications that in these lakes, the northerns follow deep-running schools of bait fish and that they cannot be relied upon to set up housekeeping. Tigers and muskies, on the other hand, seem to have well-defined areas of cover to which they return after hunting. If you fish the same water often, visit these areas in turn. Again, the object of the game is to find an area where fish often hold but are currently absent. When this happens, go look for them!

**Flies for Summer**

Northerns generally aren't selective, but in my experience, tigers and muskies can be. It is fair to say, however, that all pike can become accustomed to one kind of prey and may prefer flies that bear some resemblance to that prey, particularly in size. In the spring, when the pike need all the food they can get, a two-inch shiner may be an acceptable meal. When forage is more abundant in the warmer months, pike may refuse these small fish in favor of larger prey. So, in summer I routinely throw large (size 2/0) flies. When tied on these hooks, my divers and bunny flies may be six inches long or longer.

In clear waters, I still find black, white, and combinations of black and white tough to beat, but I also use olive/yellow flies, such as D's Minnows, and tell myself confidently that they look like baby perch. I also like white Deceivers with a black streak that I maintain look like spots and shiners. In discolored waters, I break out my brighter flies: chartreuse, yellow, orange, and combinations thereof.

Summertime pike fishing will determine just how serious you really are about catching pike on fly tackle. Many anglers pursue other species after the spring spawning season has ended, but pike have to feed, and as long as they're feeding in water that you can fish with fly tackle, you can catch them on a fly. In any case, before you know it the mornings will start getting cooler, and the sun will begin setting earlier. Then it will be time to start thinking about fall pike fishing.

# FIVE

# FALL, SLOW FISHING FOR BIG PIKE

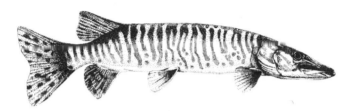

F or many people, fall is marked simply by the start of school or by Labor Day. Is Labor Day really the end of summer? Not for our purposes. In many parts of the country, summer fishing can continue for another month or two. Water holds heat well, and in large lakes the water forms a substantial heat reservoir. The kids are in school, but daytime temperatures may still be well into the eighties. Best of all for the flyfisherman, campgrounds and lakeshores begin to empty, and there is the opportunity for good late summer angling.

For our purposes, fall marks the period of time between a lake's end-of-summer turnover and when it ices over. So avoid putting what you'll learn in this chapter into practice until fall actually arrives. Enjoy the last of the summer, because the pike angler's fall is a mixed time of the year. It's a time when pike feed heavily in preparation for the winter, and it can be a great time to take large pike in lakes. But, it's also a challenging time to catch pike because, as temperatures drop, they can be difficult to reach with fly tackle. To understand why this is so, we need to look at the changes that occur to the water as the seasons change.

In spring, we fished in the shallows where the waters first became warm enough to support aquatic life. This warming process is more complex than it might at first appear, and it's worth examining in some detail. When spring arrives and the ice melts, the surface of a lake gradually warms to thirty-nine degrees, the "magic" temperature for water. At this temperature, water is at its densest. When the surface layer, the epilimnion, warms to thirty-nine degrees, it sinks, driving the cooler, deeper waters to the surface where they are warmed to thirty-nine degrees and then sink in turn. This phenomenon, known as turnover, serves to mix the waters in a lake until the entire lake reaches thirty-nine degrees. Just as significantly, the mixing of the waters also distributes the available oxygen evenly throughout the lake. Once turnover is complete, the fish in a lake can be at any depth, since the temperature is uniform. At this time, pike will begin the move to their spawning areas.

The surface waters continue to warm as spring progresses, and the warmer layer of water floats on the heavier water beneath. The lake begins to stratify. As spring changes to summer, the shallow portions of the lake become too warm for pike. The lake remains stratified, and due to the lack of mixing, the deeper, cooler waters begin to lose oxygen. Then pike are stuck between a rock and a hard place. The pike adjust to this by living more deeply in the lake, but not in the oxygen-poor greater depths.

As fall approaches, temperatures drop first in the shallows, and the epilimnion begins to cool. Because the waters in the shallows have cooled, pike return to the shallows again, feeding heavily. This is a temporary situation, one that is like the post-spawn of late spring, and you should fish this "false fall" using the same tactics and flies. The late season turnover has not occurred and the pike fisherman's fall hasn't started either.

The water continues to cool until the epilimnion finally reaches that magic thirty-nine-degree mark. Unlike water temperatures in spring, the water beneath is now warmer than the epilimnion. The dense, cool surface water once again sinks, driving lighter, warmer waters to the surface, and as it did in the spring, turnover occurs again. It may take a few days or even a few weeks, but when turnover is complete, the oxygen and temperature levels throughout the lake equalize at thirty-nine degrees.

Now we've arrived at the time of year that the pike flyfisher can appropriately call fall. The cooling process continues and the lake again stratifies. The surface waters are still warmer than the depths, and the pike will seek shallower water than in summer. This would appear to be a time for rejoicing on the part of the flyfisherman, but it isn't. In response to the approach of winter, insects aren't hatching in large numbers, and emergers aren't available to forage fish. Plants have begun to die. Small forage fish will begin searching deep for nymphs. Larger forage fish will be drawn deeper in pursuit of these smaller fish. And this will, of course, draw pike down, deeper than they would be in spring.

More so than at any other time of the year, the fall flyfisher must be aware of what is occurring in the lake. Pike will gradually return to the shallows, before turnover, as the surface waters cool. If you fish regularly, you'll notice that you're beginning to take fish in shallower water. During this time, you'll be using the spring tactics and flies we've discussed. Then, vegetation will begin to die off in the shallows, and you'll see masses of floating moss and grasses. A sudden decrease in water clarity caused by the dying vegetation and microorganisms will tell you that turnover is at hand. Enjoy the shallow-water fishing that is left to you, because it won't last much longer.

You'll notice that your fishing will become less productive. Turnover has begun, and the fish have scattered. The pike flyfisher man's fall has arrived. The turnover itself can last a few days or a few weeks. This is a good time to visit a local river and get in some fine fall pike fishing there.

## Fall Tactics

After turnover is complete, pike are more mobile than at any other time of the year. The key to good fishing, therefore, is to keep moving. You will be fishing in five to twelve feet of water. If your favorite lake has an abrupt drop-off to this depth, you may once again be able to wade safely in the shallow water along the edge of the drop-off and cast out to where the pike are cruising. However, you're more likely to do well if you fish from a boat or canoe.

The boat or canoe lesson is one that I have to relearn every year. As you've probably gathered, I like to wade for pike. Fall fishing often finds me at the edge of a drop-off, wading in just a little bit too much water. During the course of a day's fishing, as I dance around while fighting a pike or as the wind kicks up a bit of a chop, I slowly dribble a gallon or so of very cold water into my waders. People tell me that eventually I'll get too old for this nonsense and then I'll plant myself in a boat where I belong.

Virtually all of the fishing will now be subsurface, and I usually put my floating lines away at this time of the year. I make long casts and give my sink-tip or full-sink line plenty of time to do its job. Now is the time to go back to sheltered bays and work along the points. If you have a boat, fishing saddles between points can also be productive.

In fall, large fish will come back into water that is shallow (but not as shallow as in spring). These big fish are looking for substantial meals to take them through the winter, and they tend to be uninterested in

In fall, midday heat can bring forage fish and pike back in to shore. *B. Snellgrove.*

a snack. So in the fall I fish big flies; the Bunny Bugs I use at this time of the year are about seven inches long.

The size of these fall flies can surprise, even shock, other fishermen. On one occasion when I began fishing a local lake, a man fishing near me approached and asked me if I'd mind moving off a bit. He was convinced that my big Bunny Bug was scaring the fish. Wishing to keep the peace, I moved off and over the course of an hour or so landed four nice pike. As I released the last fish, I noticed that my friend had closed the gap between us considerably. It was a much humbler angler who then asked to borrow one of my "scary" flies.

Cooling waters slow fish down. That means that you should slow and smooth your retrieve. The object of the game is to make your fly look like an easy-to-grab meal. I reduce my big two- to three-foot summer strips to slower, smoother strips of perhaps twelve inches.

To find active fish, look for warmer water temperatures that will keep the pike moving and feeding. There are several things you can do to find warmer water. First, you can fish during the heat of the day. Midday heat can trigger bursts of activity, which will bring forage fish and trailing pike back in to shore. Second, you can again look for bays with dark, mucky bottoms. Remember that these bays will collect and hold heat much longer than lightly colored, sandy-bottomed bays. You can also fish the downwind sides of bays and points. If the wind is up, surface waters warmed by the sun will be pushed downwind by the breeze. Finally, you can go back to those same springs you sought out in the summer. Spring water is relatively constant in temperature. In summer, those springs provided water that was cool enough to hold pike; in fall, they provide water that is warm enough to support pike.

What you don't need at this time of the year are cold fronts, but you'll suffer through them anyway. As in spring, pike will hit more aggressively as the front moves in and will retreat to warmer, deeper water when it's present. With the trend toward cooling waters, a severe cold front may push the fish deep and keep them from coming as far back into the shallows as you'd like. Should this occur, you really have no alternative but to try to fish deeper.

If you're fortunate enough to live near lakes that hold both northerns and trout, you're in luck. In Colorado, fall marks a time of fine streamer fishing for trout in lakes. I never miss it, but I also make sure that I've got my pike tackle handy. If you've been using heavy trout gear for pike, make sure you stuff a couple of big streamers or Bunny Bugs in your vest along with some pike-class leaders. If the "trout" suddenly start stealing your #6 Muddler Minnows, switch flies and leaders—but do it quickly, because the pike are moving.

Fall is a good time to prospect the lake again. You'll begin by fishing a bit deeper than you did in the spring. In the shallows, the vegetation has already died off, and the forage fish will run deeper to find shelter and food. If you're lucky, your lake will still have growing (or dormant) vegetation in deeper waters. As a general rule, I would suggest fishing in five to twelve feet of water.

In any event, both the pike and their prey will be seeking shelter. In some cases, the first drop-off may be enough to make fish comfortable. In others, fish may seek out rocky banks or walls where they can hide. Look for banks that may drop into as much as twenty feet of water.

Finally, in the course of building many reservoirs, trees are flooded. In the summer, these trees may be too deep to provide shelter for pike or their prey. In the fall, when most reservoirs are low, they may provide excellent shelter for pike and forage fish.

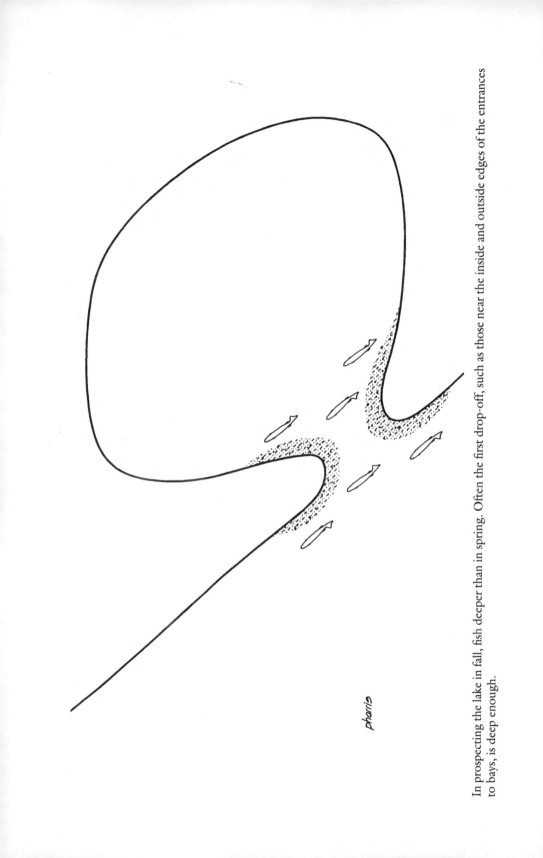

In prospecting the lake in fall, fish deeper than in spring. Often the first drop-off, such as those near the inside and outside edges of the entrances to bays, is deep enough.

**Keys to Fall Success**

There are two keys to being successful at fall pike flyfishing. The first key is to keep moving. The forage fish are deeper now, and there aren't likely to be as many nooks and crannies for them to hide in. They must keep moving, snaring nymphs and scuds when and where they can. The pike will trail along, grabbing a meal at opportune moments. The problem presented by moving pike is relatively simple to address: you keep moving, too. That's one of the reasons I recommend the use of a boat or canoe at this time of year; it greatly increases your mobility and your ability to find the fish.

Second, you must be able to get your fly down to where the pike are holding and keep it there. This is very important. The problem of getting your fly down deep can be addressed in two ways—one is relatively straightforward, the other may raise a few eyebrows.

The straightforward approach is to move to weighted flies and, at a minimum, sink-tip lines. When a subsurface fly is retrieved, it usually describes a U-shaped arc; it sinks to depth, the fisherman begins his retrieve, and the fly sails along at depth for at time and then begins its climb back to the surface as the line shortens. This is less productive in the fall because the amount of time that your fly spends in the deeper water is limited. Long, double-haul casts will help you get enough line out to broaden the "U," permitting you to keep the fly at productive depths longer. Full-sink lines will do an even better job, but they can be a pain in the neck to cast.

And what, you ask, is the unconventional approach? Many years ago, fly pattern books regularly featured large patterns that were described as trolling flies. Fishermen cast sinking lines and either drifted along with the wind or paddled their boat to give the fly some action. This technique worked fine then and it works fine now. It also addresses precisely the needs of fall pike fishing: it keeps the fly running at depth and it allows you to cover a large amount of water. Many flyfishermen will protest that this isn't flyfishing, feeling perhaps that simply sitting in a boat and dragging a fly around violates the purity of our sport. That might be correct, if that was all that this technique consisted of. Remember that most of our large streamers produce little inherent action that will attract a fish. Modern exceptions to this rule are flies like the Edgewater Wiggler and the wool/silicone rubber patterns that feature molded lips that impart lifelike action to the fly. But most of the time, when we fish a streamer in a conventional manner, we impart action to the fly with judicious strips of line and twitches of the rod.

A boat greatly increases your mobility and your ability to find fish. *B. Snellgrove.*

If you elect to wind-drift a streamer for pike, you will still have to impart action to the fly in the same manner. In a canoe, I do this by paddling a stroke or two and permitting the canoe to coast for a bit while I twitch and pull the rod in what I hope is a convincing manner. Remember that speed is not of the essence; the waters have cooled, and both the pike and their prey have slowed down. In addition, too much speed can make the line plane, raising it above productive depths.

One of my favorite places to fish for pike is the Boundary Waters Canoe Area. Power boats are banned, and only those resolute (or crazy) souls willing to portage their gear and canoe from lake to lake really get a chance to experience this marvelous, pristine wilderness area, to be eaten alive by black flies and mosquitoes, and to catch the big pike that live there. I routinely drag a Bunny Bug behind my canoe as I paddle and I take fish often enough to make me continue the practice religiously. You might wonder how I manage to paddle and handle a rod at the same time. Actually, this is a nagging little detail that I'm still working on. Friends who have witnessed this process tell me that there is nothing more pleasant than watching me drop a paddle and grab frantically for a disappearing rod while trying desperately to avoid capsizing my gear-filled canoe. When I invite them to try my tactics, they generally decline. I think they feel that the process is like walking barefoot over hot coals: more fun to watch than it is to do. In any case, I'll leave the decision about whether or not this activity is "real" flyfishing to you. I'll be too busy catching fish from my canoe to worry much about it.

At some point during your fishing endeavors, fall will finally give way to winter. The shallow bays will freeze and the thought of spending a day in a boat or up to your hips in ice water will (or should!) become less appealing. That's winter, folks, and it's time to dig out the vise and prepare for the coming of spring.

### Flies for Fall

Fly selection for fall pike flyfishing is based on three factors:

1. Subsurface flies are a must. You'll be covering lots of water with sinking lines. Anything that you can do to get the fly and line to depth quickly will permit you to cover water faster. Flies tied with bulky materials that impede sinking or flies that have a lot of inherent buoyancy will slow the process.
2. The pike you find after turnover are likely to be large fish, the ones that prefer cooler temperatures. This means you'll want to use large flies. Size 2/0, seven-inch-long flies are relatively standard.
3. In many lakes, turnover is marked by a definite decrease in water clarity. Bright colors will make your flies easier for pike to see.

One of my standbys for pike fishing is the Bunny Bug, but because the bulky rabbit skin impedes sinking, you may have to tie your fall Bunny Bugs with some lead wire. Although a standard Bunny Bug will certainly sink, lead will help it sink quickly. Adding lead can make a fly that is already a heavy, awkward affair to cast a real nightmare, especially on trout gear. On the other hand, Bunny Bugs are still very effective flies. I suggest that if you're a good caster and you've upgraded to nine-weight or heavier gear, by all means tie and try some weighted Bunny Bugs. And, if you are willing to try trolling, the Bunny Bug can be a very effective choice, indeed.

A more practical fly for this time of year is a big, fast-sinking streamer. Large Deceivers, brightly colored tarpon flies, bucktails, matukas, featherwings, eelworm streamers, and large leech patterns are all good producers. I don't believe that this is because the fish especially prefer them. Rather, I think it is because I can get them to an appropriate depth quickly and keep them running there, which allows me to cover more water.

If you're blessed with clear water, black, white, and combinations thereof are tough to beat. If you're not (and you probably won't be), it's time to break out brighter colors. All of the fluorescent colors can be effective, as can other bright colors such as reds, yellows, and oranges. This is also a time to experiment with contrasting, even clashing, colors, such as yellow/black, chartreuse/orange, and red/white. You might also ask at local fishing stores to determine if the spin fishermen have noticed that the pike seem to have a color preference. This can be a basis to help you choose the color of your fly.

True fall fishing, the fishing that takes place after turnover, admittedly can be slow. In fact, it may be slow enough that it simply isn't for you. For me, the payoff comes from being able to fish quiet, deserted lakes, the fact that larger pike are once again accessible, and the opportunity to be outdoors during a beautiful, invigorating time of the year. And before you give up, remember that the autumn, with its gorgeous scenery, can be a fine time to float a gentle river in search of pike.

# SIX

# OL' MAN RIVER

Rivers are magnets, drawing fishermen who like the hypnotic quality of the moving water, the sounds, and the change in the character of the water as it passes through riffles, runs, flats, and pools. And of course, most flyfishermen enjoy reading water to determine where fish may be holding.

Pike can be as much at home in rivers as in lakes, and there are some real advantages to fishing for them there. First, just as other fish prefer to avoid fighting the current, pike also seek shelter from moving water. Knowing this, the angler can read the water and concentrate on productive areas. Second, pike holding areas in rivers are rarely very deep, and flyfishermen can fish most of the water effectively without sinking lines and weighted flies. Finally, rivers do not stratify. With all of the water in a river at nearly the same temperature, pike will hold in roughly the same locations throughout the year.

When I talk about a pike river, I'm referring to water with moderate currents and riffles, runs, and pools along its length. Large rivers, such as the Mississippi, with stretches of deep, still water are essentially long lakes as far as flyfishing for pike is concerned. Small, steep-gradient streams, like your favorite brookie water, move too fast to support pike.

Instead, an ideal pike river is wide enough, slow enough, and deep enough to make a float trip pleasant, rather than terrifying. In many cases, it will be a river into which pike have strayed from a connecting lake. This ideal pike river will have calm shallows where pike can spawn and large pools or backwaters where they can cruise in search of food. It will also have more and bigger areas of cover than those that we

Drifting until you reach a good area gives the advantages of floating and wading. *P. Framsted.*

typically associate with trout streams, for instance, because pike do not do well in waters where they have to constantly fight the current.

In lake fishing, as you've learned, finding pike is one of the most challenging parts of the sport. It's considerably easier to find pike in a river. Relatively shallow water and consistent temperatures mean that pike are not forced to move around due to temperature changes. Pike will move to spawning grounds or to areas that hold more food, but otherwise they are likely to be found in the same places throughout the year. Fast water serves to localize pike in areas where they can escape the current. In general, the fish you catch are likely to be found in one of three places: spawning grounds, in deep pools or slack water, or in "lies" in faster current where they can hold until prey happens by. With a little practice, you can become adept at locating pike lies in a river.

Although you can certainly wade-fish for pike, floating a river will permit you to cover substantial amounts of water in a very comfortable manner. It is not at all unusual to cover ten or more miles of water during a day's float trip. I like to drift along, casting to places that may hold pike until I catch one or until I reach a large pool that warrants more thorough attention. Then I beach the canoe and wade the area.

Floating a river in a boat, raft, or canoe also permits you to carry more gear than you normally would. In Colorado, we're fortunate to have several rivers that contain both pike and trout. In eastern states, pike often share rivers with smallmouth bass and bluegill. With a boat, it's simple to carry both light trout or panfish tackle and pike gear, to say nothing of rain suits, the fixings for a fancy shore lunch, and cameras.

In Alaska, very large pike are regularly taken in the lower tributaries of the Yukon River. In Kentucky, pike can be found in the Licking and Green rivers. In Colorado, the Yampa, Rio Grande, Conejos, and South Platte rivers all offer good habitat for pike. Massachusetts's only natural pike fishery is the Connecticut River. The odds are that there is good pike fishing in a river near you. Look for more information about pike rivers in your area in the appendix.

### Pike Lies

I'm sure you've heard the old joke that asks the question, "Where do gorillas sleep?" The answer, of course, is, "Anywhere they want to." The same is true for pike. Where do pike live in the river? Anywhere they want to. These are big, tough fish, and they can easily drive competing trout or bass from the lies they prefer. This isn't as tough on the losing fish as you might think. As a rule, they are smaller and can make do with other lies. Trout, for example, can live in heavier current than a pike can tolerate. In locating pike in a river, you'll

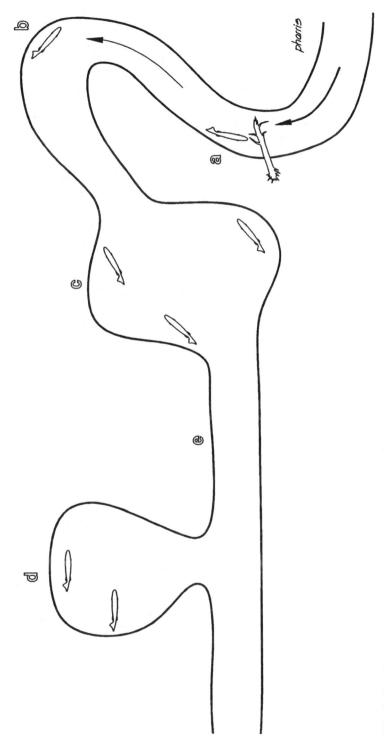

Pike find shelter from the river current behind a submerged tree (a), at an undercut bank (b), in slow pools (c), and in sloughs (d). They avoid stretches of fast water (e).

have to learn to think like a pike, remembering that the fish you're trying to think like is the toughest kid on the block. As you might expect, it will make the very best lies its own.

A pike has two main requirements for its lie. First, as a big fish, it requires some room. Second, a pike will want to live in water that is as slow as possible. Therefore, the quiet water behind a small rock and the little pool that attract trout and trout fishermen probably won't produce pike for you. In an area where current is present, a pike must have more shelter than a trout requires, and small pools won't do the job. A few feet of undercut bank on the outside of a sharp bend in the river may be too small to hold a pike, but a similar area on the outside of a long, gentle bend may be large enough to be just what a pike is looking for.

Stretches of flat water that give pike room to hunt are also appealing to them. In those slack-water areas, a pike will still want to hide. If the water is slow enough to produce weed beds, look for pike in them. Many times materials carried down during run-off will settle out in slow water, forming brush piles and sand bars. These areas can be very productive.

This is not to say that you should ignore faster water. In those areas, look for large objects that block a substantial amount of the current. On a stretch of one of my favorite Colorado rivers, I've snaked pike on several occasions from the back seat of a submerged '57 DeSoto. The first time I hooked a pike in the car, I was casting across the river and retrieving through a deep pool upstream from the car. I stopped my retrieve for a moment to admire a wild turkey gobbling in the field bordering the river. While I gawked at the bird, the current swept my fly into the car and around one of the window pillars. Naturally, that's when the biggest pike I'd ever seen in the river came up from the back seat and belted the fly. With the line wrapped around the pillar, getting the fish in was out of the question. To make matters worse, the pool was too deep to wade.

For a moment, I gave serious consideration to going swimming, but while I thought the matter over, the pike slipped off. The lost fish did teach me a lesson, as so many lost fish do. Now, the thicker the cover, no matter how improbable, the more carefully I watch that fly! And when I fish that particular river, I always take a moment to fire a fly into the car.

### Spring River Fishing

For our purposes, we'll consider spring to be the time from the melting of the ice on the river to the end of run-off. The same kinds of pre-spawn, spawn, and post-spawn behaviors that marked spring pike fishing in lakes will take place.

Before we go any further, remember that spring means fast, high, icy waters. Across the country, people are killed every year because they attempt to float rivers during heavy spring rains or run-off. To avoid becoming a statistic, I urge you to talk to state game officials in your area before you float any rivers in the spring. They'll be able to tell you when it's safe. As you'll see, because of the behavior of pike at this time of the year, it may not be necessary for you to float the river at all.

As soon as the ice leaves the river, pike will become active. Just as is the case with their lake-bound brethren, they will feed heavily to develop the bulk that will carry them through the stresses of the spawning season. As the water warms, the stream comes to life— insects emerge and vegetation begins to grow. Forage fish start working the shallows in search of food, and the pike follow. Because the waters are low and slow, pike may inhabit areas of the river that, later in the season, would be too swift for them to survive in. They will also be hungry and may be willing to inhabit faster waters than they would normally if this means that their chances of snaring a meal are improved.

During this time, concentrate on holding areas where the pike can find shelter from the current and dart out to find food. Pools are an excellent choice at this time of year, as are stretches of flat water where the current is very moderate. Look for areas where pike can hide: brush piles, clumps of boulders, and miscellaneous junk that may have been placed along the riverbank to prevent erosion (old cars and tires, for example).

Eventually, run-off will begin. The river will rise and low-lying streamside areas may be flooded. Work your way out of the riverbed with the rising waters. Secondary channels may flood at this time of the year and can be excellent places to find pike. Sloughs and flooded meadows and pastures can also be good producers. All these areas provide the pike with the only thing that they may have lacked in the river: a shallow, calm, weedy area in which to spawn. They will seek out areas of flooded vegetation covered by a foot or so of water and will take advantage of these temporary spawning grounds, happily spawning over weeds and brush.

Sloughs and flooded meadows can also be good producers. *B. Snellgrove.*

For the flyfisherman, timing is everything. Some years run-off will come early enough to permit the pike to move into flooded shallow areas some weeks before they actually spawn. In this case, you'll have an exciting pre-spawn season, just as you do in lakes. Other years, the run-off will occur later, and when the pike move into the flooded areas, they will be ready to spawn and reluctant to strike. To help your planning, state game agencies often keep records detailing when fish spawn in the rivers and lakes they manage. In addition, they may be able to make an educated guess about how an unusually warm or cold spring will affect pike spawning behavior.

As you will remember, in lakes post-spawn females quit feeding for a period of time. They may leave the shallows to recover from spawning, or they may simply be unresponsive. After they've recovered, they resume feeding with the males who remained in shallow water. Both sexes then feed heavily until rising temperatures drive them into deeper water. Pike follow the same pattern in rivers, but it's not rising temperatures that drives them from the shallows. It's dropping water levels. The spawning shallows, usually created by run-off, are temporary by nature. Again, timing is everything, and if you're lucky, run-off will last long enough to permit the females to resume feeding with the males. A long run-off, so dreaded by trout flyfishermen, is great for flyfishermen after river pike.

If you're not so lucky, run-off will conclude, and falling water will force the males back in the riverbed before the females can return. Of course, you'll still be able to find the pike easily, since the holding areas they will go to are well defined and within reach of fly tackle. In either case, the pike will still be in the post-spawn season and will hit eagerly.

If you're fortunate enough to have the sort of spring that will permit you to fish the shallows in both pre- and post-spawn conditions, you should fish likely areas as carefully as you would spawning areas in lakes. The pike may hold in very shallow water, so plan on fishing in just inches of water. The likelihood of being able to sight-fish to pike is very good if the water is clear. The bad news is that rising waters may put the pike in some horrible places. Flooded thickets and woods are fine places to catch pike in the spring, but miserable places to cast to them. Short, lobbing casts and bow-and-arrow casts may be the order of the day, an awkward situation to say the least. If you can put up with it, you may be rewarded with large fish. If the fish are in heavy cover, this is the time to switch to heavy leaders, so you can stop the pike before it knots your line firmly around a bush.

## Spring Flies

My choice of spring flies for pike is based on the nature of the area I'll be fishing. Because pre- and post-spawn pike are very active, virtually anything large enough to get their attention will work, but remember where you're likely to be fishing: in brush, flooded thickets, and stubble. You're certain to lose some flies, and for my money, if you're going to lose flies, you should lose flies that are quick and cheap to tie.

Therefore, I tend to use a lot of cork or foam-headed popping bugs and Bunny Bugs. I can lose a half dozen of these flies in an outing and replace them when I get home in an hour or so. Fancy clipped-hair poppers and divers take more time to replace, so I'm less willing to chance losing them.

The water is likely to be murky, if not downright muddy, so highly visible flies are a must. This is the time for bright colors; shades of chartreuse, orange, yellow, and red have all been productive for me. If you have some spare time, you might consider putting an existing fly back in the vise long enough to attach some Krystal Flash, Flashabou, silver mylar, or other material that will give it more sparkle.

## Summer River Fishing

Summer flyfishing in rivers begins when the pike return from the flooded shallows to their holding areas in the riverbed. It's probably safe for you to assume that the pike will remain in their holding areas for the balance of the summer. Although the river will warm as the summer progresses, there will be none of the stratification that occurs in lakes, forcing pike to move to cooler, more comfortable water.

If the river you're fishing is used for irrigation purposes, water levels may fluctuate during the course of the summer. When you're fishing during low-water conditions you should take the opportunity to scan the banks between the water and the high-water mark. This way you'll be able to spot likely pike holding areas that will be under water when the river is full. Holding areas change from year to year as rushing waters move things around and deposit other materials along the banks.

Just as in lakes, summer marks a return to normalcy for pike. They hold in their lies, often in the company of other pike of the same size. They dart out from cover to grab a passing fish and then return. This is very similar to the behavior of pike in lakes, with one exception. Lake pike cruise to find food, holing-up from time to time to await prey. In many cases, this behavior is not practical for river pike. A journey of any consequence would mean a trip through fast water, which they prefer to avoid. If you float a river several times during a season, always cast to areas that have been productive in the past. The chances are good fish are still calling the area home.

## Float Fishing

By this time, the rushing torrents of spring have given way to smoother, calmer summer waters. I hope you'll take advantage of this and float a river, both because it's a good way to cover a lot of water and because it's simply a nice way to see some country. As that country is rolling past and when I'm not gaping at something of interest, I cast to holding areas, such as small pools, that experience tells me may only hold a single pike. When a good-sized deadfall appears around a bend of the river or when I come to a large pool, it's time to run the boat to shore and begin wading. This is the real benefit of floating rivers. You have the ability to cover significant amounts of water and still work areas thoroughly.

Remember that a pike is the toughest kid on the block and will take the best lies. *P. Framsted*.

There are three reasons for this kind of ride-and-wade approach. The first has to do with water temperature. The river will generally be uniform in temperature, so in a pool or an area of slack water, a pike can be cruising anywhere within the confines of the slow water. It pays to work the area thoroughly. The second has to do with the limited number of holding areas available on rivers. Very often several pike will have to share one deadfall or one small pool. So if you catch a nice pike from a brush pile, you should definitely cast there again.

The third reason has to do with a facet of summer pike behavior we see in lakes. You'll recall that a pike that has recently eaten a meal may sulk and refuse your fly. Pike in any holding area may consist both of fish that have eaten and are unlikely to strike and of fish that are ready for a meal. You may see a pike basking in the sun, helping his digestion along. The pike you're after, the hungry one, may be hiding a bit deeper in the brush. So work those brush piles and other holding areas thoroughly. This requires repeated, accurate casts, and is easier to do when you're wading.

This kind of fishing also means that you'll be casting into areas that are natural fly-traps, areas where, after you hook it, a pike can dart back into the brush or weeds, hopelessly snarling your leader. One way to address this problem is to use heavier leaders. When the pike hits, you'll be able to "cross his eyes" and move the fish out into open water quickly. Another way to combat the problem is to use floating flies. If the pike are willing to take floaters, they'll have to come to the surface. That will allow you to move the fish out into open water. Once you've got the fish in open water, it will often run for the depths, which makes fighting it much easier.

Now I'm going to make trout flyfishermen very happy. A substantial portion of their fishing time is spent avoiding, overcoming, and swearing at drag. They'll be glad to know that pike don't care about drag. Feel free to swim your fly in whatever manner will best present it to a pike. In fact, I suggest the same kind of rapid retrieve that you use in a lake. Dead drifts and figure-eight retrieves have never worked for me on river pike.

## Summer Flies

Summertime in rivers marks a time of stability. Unless unusual agricultural demands are placed on the river or there are heavy rains, water levels are generally consistent. Water clarity is usually dramatically improved from spring run-off conditions.

If you've been using wire leader systems, now is the time to switch to hard-monofilament systems. While the brightly colored flies you used during the spring may still produce for you, I recommend giving both white and black patterns a try. Finally, rivers often have fewer varieties of pike food than do lakes. In some of our mountain rivers, for example, the six- to seven-inch meal menu is limited to suckers, whitefish, and trout. Should this be the case in your local rivers, it makes sense to tie some Deceiver-type patterns that imitate the prevalent prey species. Pike aren't selective in the way trout are, but it can't hurt to make your offering look like a familiar meal, particularly if the variety of food available is limited.

Floating or diver flies also have a definite place in your summer pike fly selection. As I mentioned above, they can permit you to work deadfall and other difficult holding areas while reducing the risk of snags. More so than in lakes, river pike are likely to be at shallow depths where they can be persuaded to come up for a floating fly. Finally, floating flies are lighter than their sinking counterparts.

Especially if you're using trout gear, the ease of casting lighter flies and line may be important to you.

## Fall River Fishing

Rivers are probably the best places to catch pike in the fall. As we've seen, lake-dwelling pike are often more difficult to catch because of the effects of turnover, and since they have warmer waters available to them in the depths of the lake, they will eventually move beyond the reach of the flyfisher. The situation in rivers is much simpler: all the water in the river gets colder, and finally it freezes. Before ice ends the season, river fishing for pike can be great. Generally, the water level is low. This reduces the overall size of the river and concentrates pike in the holding areas. Like the pike that live in lakes, river pike will feed heavily in the fall as they prepare for the rigors of winter.

Once again, it is a fine time to float a river, especially if you can schedule the trip so that you can enjoy the fall foliage. You'll be looking for the same kinds of holding areas that you sought out during the summer months. These areas are likely to be significantly smaller than they were in the summer because water levels are low, but they may hold even more pike.

Because the pike will be feeding heavily and grabbing meals anywhere they can, it pays to be prepared to work a fly at any depth. If you'll be in a boat, it should be relatively easy for you to carry two rods, one equipped with floating line and a floating fly or diver for use in quiet shallows and brush piles, the other equipped with full-sink or sink-tip line and a streamer for working deeper pools. This is, of course, a good idea for spring and summer pike fishing, too.

Just as in the summer, I recommend a ride-and-wade approach. The pike will be even more concentrated, and you should work likely areas thoroughly. Falling water temperatures will eventually slow the pike's metabolism, so you should concentrate your fishing in the warmest hours of the day and slow your retrieves as winter nears.

## Fall Flies

Just as is the case in lakes, there may be a die-off of vegetation in the fall of the year. For a time, this could result in a decrease in water clarity, and under those conditions you should again fish your brightly colored spring patterns in fluorescent and bright primary colors. The addition of tinsel, mylar, Flashabou, or Krystal Flash may also help. In lakes, the dead vegetation may suspend for days or even weeks. In rivers, the material is carried downstream by the current, and the last weeks of fall are often marked by extremely clear water. When this happens, switch back to white and black patterns.

At this time of the year, I consider a hard-monofilament leader system a must because it is much less visible. You may also discover that you have to reduce your shock tippet by a size or two, as well, again to make it less visible. Don't worry, by this time, you'll be such an experienced pike flyfisherman that you'll be able to take pike on lighter leaders.

Whether you fish rivers or lakes, experience is the key to success. As you spend more time flyfishing for pike, you will become more proficient at it. At some point, you'll want to start thinking about a trip to a place where the big pike lie like a forest of sunken logs. The remote Canadian lakes will be calling you.

# SEVEN

# OH, CANADA!

E very flyfisherman has a dream. For trout flyfishers, that dream might be a trip to New Zealand for monster browns. For Pacific salmon anglers, Alaska looms large in their thoughts. Saltwater fly-fishermen stare off into space and dream of the Keys. And pike flyfishermen dream of Canada and its giant lakes.

You already know that pike like bays. Well, imagine pike-packed bays larger than most American lakes, bays found in lakes that encompass hundreds of thousands of surface acres. I've fished minor bays of Canadian lakes that are larger than any of the lakes we have in Colorado. Every key element that the pike need is present in these bays: fat forage fish in the form of whitefish and young lake trout, cool temperatures that suit the needs of big pike, and vast expanses of weedy, shallow water. Trophy northerns literally stack up in these shallow bays. Remote Canadian waters represent the best chance a flyfisherman has to catch a pike of over thirty pounds.

Canadian lakes are simply tailor-made to the needs of big pike. Ample supplies of forage fish and cool temperatures allow pike to live longer and therefore grow larger than their cousins to the south. Because many of the lakes are genuinely remote, fishing pressure is very limited, and the fishing season is short, lasting only three months or so. The best part may be that many of Canada's trophy pike areas are limited to catch-and-release fishing. Regulations mandate single, barbless-hook fishing—even for spin fishermen—in many of these areas. Our neighbors to the north have created a monument to strict conservation policies and have thereby assured quality fishing for years to come. As these waters prove, fishing could be improved almost everywhere, if only more people believed that pure waters and catch-and-release fishing benefit everyone in the long run.

One of the saddest things I see is a group of fishermen headed home with a limit of fish, far too many fish for even a large fish dinner. Those fish are going into the bowels of a freezer, where the quality of the meat will deteriorate far below that of the farm-raised fish available at a grocery store. I'd like to know how much of that frozen fish eventually ends up in the garbage. On the other hand, maybe I wouldn't.

I love fresh fish for dinner, and a shore lunch forms a memorable part of many fishing trips. But our harvest of this resource should always be tempered by the realization that we live for a short period of time and that it is our duty to pass on fishing resources to those who come after us that are at least as good, and hopefully better, than the ones we've enjoyed. Canadian regulations help make sure this will be the case.

### Getting There

Year after year, I return to northern Manitoba. By going back to the same place I'm missing out on an opportunity to tour a vast, beautiful country. By all means, explore all the options available to you in Canada. I can only say that in my case, big pike, and plenty of them, lure me back to Manitoba each year. One of my favorite areas is Nejalini Lodge on Nejalinini Lake in Manitoba. (No, I'm not sure why the name of the lodge and the lake are spelled differently.) This is a pristine lake in a fabulous tundra setting. Lodge owner Marvin Benson states, and rightly so, that many portions of this lake have never seen a hook. Mind-boggling numbers of giant northerns, lake trout, and grayling are caught and released here every year. Again, let me emphasize that the terrific flyfishing I have in Manitoba is by no means unique; it's just the Canadian experience I'm most familiar with.

To get there, I board an airplane in Denver and fly to Minneapolis, where I board another airplane and fly to Winnipeg, where I transfer to charter aircraft and fly to the lodge. By the time this process is over, I'm about seven-hundred miles north of anywhere. The cost of my week's stay includes virtually everything: meals, boat, motor, gas, and guide—and very large northern pike. I'm responsible for my personal gear, tackle, and the like. Alcoholic beverages and tobacco are also extra-cost items, of course.

In fairness to the rest of your family, I recommend considering carefully whether your Canadian trip should be a family vacation.

Getting seven hundred miles from nowhere. *B. Snellgrove.*

A fly-in trip to Canada is a great parent-child trip and is a fabulous way for a group of friends to enjoy the outdoors. Typically, fly-in lodges are equipped like a good hotel. The facilities, food, scenery, and comradeship are simply first rate. However, you should bear in mind that tourist attractions (e.g., video games, fast food, and shopping) are simply not to be had in remote areas. If your family needs these things, I would recommend a solo trip and a separate family vacation.

When you plan this kind of trip, remember that you really are a thousand miles from anywhere and that you're a flyfisherman, a rather rare breed where you'll be going. Therefore, don't count on anything being available in the event that you break tackle, run out of flies, or tear a hole in your waders. If you're not prepared for disaster, you could spend the last few days of your trip wishing you had been. With all this in mind, some suggestions are listed later in this chapter for gear, tackle, and consumables you'll need.

When you fish these Canadian waters, you'll have the benefit of a guide. Generally, he or she will be knowledgeable and will be able to put you on to fish. However, the odds are also high that your guide will never have guided a flyfisherman before. So, before you choose a lodge, make sure they are receptive. They might prefer to cater to spin fishers.

After you've arrived at the lodge but before you go out on the water, take the time to talk matters over with your guide. Take a few minutes to show him how far you can cast, and if you're going to wade, let him know the depths you're comfortable with. Spin and bait fishers may have trouble keeping their heavy hardware out of the weeds, and your guide may be accustomed to putting them over deeper water. Take a bit of time to show him that you can run your diver or Bunny Bug right across the tops of the weeds, even in very shallow water. Likewise, show him the kind of sink-rates and depths you can achieve with sinking lines and weighted flies. Effective communication with your guide at an early stage of the game can prevent much frustration for both you and your guide.

**Spring in Canada**

Springtime in Canada is a great time to flyfish for pike. With luck, a Canada-bound pike fisherman can enjoy two springs, the first on his home lake in the United States, the second in northern Canada. Your timing is critical. Northern Canadian lakes regularly have ice on them until mid-June or early July. In my experience, the best time to be in Canada is the first two or three weeks after the ice leaves the bays (there still may be substantial quantities of ice on the main body of the lake). Just as in the United States, pike move into shallow bays to spawn and feed, but the bays in Canada are huge, and there are many, many pike.

During my last trip to Canada in July, my partner and I caught 150 northerns in one memorable six-and-a-half-hour period. Forty-three of these fish were trophy fish (in Canada, pike over forty-two inches). Our guide took us into a small bay within a much larger one. The water was high and we were casting into willow thickets. We were wading in knee-deep water and casting into much shallower water.

We were like a couple of target shooters, firing our big flies at waiting pike. Many times, large pike would race each other in an effort to be the first to grab our flies. Even more exciting, on a couple of occasions when one of us had hooked a pike, the other was able to cast to the "losing" pike and succeed in hooking it. Then we'd have two furious pike within a few feet of each other. The fish simply wore us out. I'm not going to pretend that all of the fish we caught were twenty-five-pound monsters; only about a third of them were. The rest of them were "puny" ten- and fifteen-pound fish. The end of the day found my companion and I in awe of the size and strength of the fish we'd been catching. We also needed a night's sleep to rest our aching arms.

A pike must be over forty-two inches to be a trophy in Canada. This one was about forty-six inches with a twenty-one-inch girth! *B. Snellgrove.*

Obviously, the timing of our trip was perfect. You can do the same. Get on the telephone, write letters to lodges and Canadian fish and game agencies, and read as much as you can. Attend outdoor shows and talk to lodge owners. Eventually, you'll know when the prime post-spawn season usually occurs in the area you intend to visit.

I haven't mentioned spring turnover as a factor in your planning. That's because many lakes in northern Canada don't warm to the point where turnover occurs—although the shallow portions of large bays can become quite warm. For example, on one occasion when we were catching post-spawn pike in a shallow secondary bay fed by a creek, the water temperature was fifty-eight degrees. In the middle of the main bay, the temperature was in the low forties. In the body of the lake, lots of slushy ice was present, keeping temperatures far below the thirty-nine degrees required for turnover to occur.

Since the lakes tend to be very large, plan on covering a lot of water. Your guide will certainly help with this process. In all likelihood, your guide will take you to large shallow bays—bays that could qualify as lakes in their own right. This is where the difference between fly tackle and conventional gear will give you an advantage. Your guide may want to keep you in the bay proper. The water will be a bit deeper there, and it's easier for spin fishermen to work the water (and for him to keep the boat moving). On the other hand, you'll want him to take you into secondary bays fed by small creeks that trickle across the tundra and supply the lake with warmer water. The water in these secondary bays will be even shallower, the temperatures even warmer, the spawning situation even better, and the northerns even bigger. All of this is just right for a wading flyfisherman. The first time I went to Canada and fished these secondary bays, I was astounded to see literally hundreds of twenty-pound pike stacked up in them. The fish were often in less than a foot of water.

As you know, temperature plays a crucial role in all of this, and in Canada, temperature swings can be dramatic. During one of my trips, we had three days of temperatures in the seventies, and we caught lots of fish in knee-deep water. The next day, the temperature fell to the forties, and it rained hard. We went back to our bay, and although we still found small fish in the shallows, we had to move out into eight to ten feet of water to find large pike. They were still very aggressive and still easy to reach with a fly rod. We didn't even switch to sinking lines, we just used longer leaders. A few days of warm weather followed by a cold snap is very typical of northern lakes.

Because Canadian lakes never get very warm, a cold front doesn't produce a drastic change in water temperature. In the United States, a cold snap can drive pike into depths where they can no longer be reached with fly tackle. They can afford to sulk for a couple of days;

there will be many more warm days to come. Due to the short growing season in the Far North, pike there must take advantage of every
feeding day available to them, and typically they will resist being driven very deep for very long.

For comfort, you should be prepared for temperatures down to
the high thirties with the possibility rain or sleet. You should also
remember that the days are *long*. We usually rise at six and are on the
water by seven in the morning. We fish until suppertime, return to
the lodge to eat, and then often go back to the lake until as late as
eleven in the evening—in broad daylight! With fifteen hours of flyfishing available (as long as your stamina holds out), you'll catch a
lot of fish!

### Summer in Canada

In deep lakes in northern Canada, pike can typically be found in
shallow water, rarely more than ten feet deep, all summer long. Often,
they will be found in water less than five feet deep, which is perfect
for flyfishermen. On these lakes, there really is no spring or summer
in the sense that we've talked about previously. Pike move from post-
spawn to business as usual behavior in water that is very stable in temperature. This is very good news for flyfishermen.

If there's bad news, it's that spawning will be over in summer, and
the pike won't be concentrated. They will scatter throughout the
bays. You'll have to cover more water, but in Canada it's shallow
water that you can fish efficiently. Because the bays are big, you'll find
that fishing from a boat is the best way to travel. Fish the edges of the
bays, openings into main and secondary bays, and in the case of especially shallow areas, even the middle of the bay. You'll want to fish in
shallower water than you would in the United States in summer. It's
unlikely that Canadian pike will ever be in water over twenty feet
deep, even in the heat of summer. With this modification to your tactics in mind, you should be able to put what you've learned in the preceding chapters of this book to use.

In much of northern Canada, there really is no fall pike season in
the sense that we in the United States are used to. Because of the short
growing season, pike move into the shallows, spawn, and then eat
heavily until ice drives them into deeper water. For our purposes, in
many Canadian lakes there are really two seasons: spawn/post-spawn
and eat-like-mad-till-the-ice-comes. Pike hit flies readily through both
of them.

## Flies for Canada

In the Canadian lakes that I've fished, the waters are usually clear, and unweighted Bunny Bugs tied in black or white are definite winners. That is not to say that I don't carry an assortment of other colors. The winds that accompany a fast-moving front can produce enough chop to muddy the shallows, and brighter colors and fluorescents can be effective when this happens. Also, on several occasions I've gone back over water that I covered very thoroughly with a white Bunny Bug using a yellow/red Bunny Bug. For some reason, the yellow/red fly has always kicked up a couple of additional fish for me.

For surface fishing, large deer hair bugs, known informally as "horse poppers," are tough to beat, as are Umpqua's Swimming Baitfish flies. Any of the large, hairy mouse patterns will often provoke a vicious response. Another good choice for surface work are long, thin pencil-style bluefish poppers.

There is one caveat: all pike beat up flies badly, and really big northerns are exceptionally good at it. Either plan to carry lots of deer hair flies for surface work or tie foam-headed versions. They will stand up to the abuse a big northern metes out. Naturally, there is a tradeoff: foam is heavier than deer hair, so the more durable foam-headed flies will be a bit more cranky to cast than their deer-hair counterparts. On the plus side, they're not nearly as difficult to cast as a wet Bunny Bug.

## Gear for Canada

If at all possible, you want to be on the water during the great post-spawn season. Temperatures may range from the thirties to the seventies. During my 1992 trip, we crunched our boats through large areas of ice in July so I go prepared for virtually any kind of weather. I freely admit that I pack heavily. I also admit that I like being warm and dry. For me, the ability to layer clothing to meet changing conditions and to get into dry clothing at the end of the day is crucial for comfort. I'm a far better fisherman when I'm comfortable than when I'm not.

Besides the usual clothing, I recommend a *good* rain suit. When you need a rain suit in Canada, you really need a rain suit. Buy a good one. I also use my hooded Gore-Tex windbreaker a lot. Other cold weather gear that's important to me are fingerless gloves, a knit ski hat, and long underwear. I pack an extra set of "boat shoes" and I take a waterproof bag to carry my gear in the boat. If you're big or hard to fit, you should bring your own personal flotation device. Being stuffed into a too-small lifejacket is a lousy way to spend the day.

As I indicated earlier, it's important to have backups for your tackle. I consider the following inventory of rods to be basic: two nine-foot, nine-weight rods; one nine-foot, six-weight rod (great fun for hammer handles, rainbows, and whitefish); and one nine-foot, four-weight rod (for grayling).

For your heavy tackle, consider carrying two complete reel setups, spare spools and all. If budgetary concerns preclude this, then at a minimum carry enough spare parts to be able to re-build a drag if you have to, and don't forget the tools to do the job. I'd also recommend practicing the procedure at home a few times to make sure you've got it down pat.

I used to carry spinning rods with me to Canada. Don't worry, they weren't for pike. I'd been told there were big lake trout to be had, and that they hold too deep to reach easily with fly tackle. It's true there are big lake trout, but it's not true that they are out of

I used to carry spinning gear for big lake trout, but they can be caught on fly rods easily in Canada. *B. Snellgrove.*

reach of flyfishermen. Every year I catch many big lake trout in the shallows on my fly rod.

I also carry lots of "consumables," those things that I use up or might break or lose on a trip. These include: pre-made pike leaders (at least four replacements for each day), plus leader material to make more; flies, at least a dozen of each of my favorite patterns and colors; a vise, tools, and materials to tie more if I have to; bug dope; sun screen; and film. If you use a modern camera that is useless when the batteries die, add extra batteries

At least one spare pair of polarized sunglasses is a must. If you wear corrective lenses, definitely pack a spare pair of glasses. Contact lens wearers should do the same. If you've invested in a pair of polarized prescription glasses, back them up with polarized clip-ons.

As you know, I like to wade for pike. In cold Canadian waters, neoprene waders are the only way to go. At a minimum, pack a good repair kit for your waders. You might even consider packing a spare pair of the low-buck neoprene waders available from mail order houses.

I unhook almost all pike barehanded. I also bleed a lot. In chapter 10, I'll give you some ideas to help keep your bleeding to a minimum. If you're not prepared to suffer for your trophy pike, jaw-spreaders ease this task, and a pair of needle-nosed pliers will make your life even more pleasant. This is no job for a wimpy hemostat. If you elect to use tools, either make sure you don't drop your pliers and/or spreader in the drink or pack a spare of each.

I always plan on at least one day of weather that is so miserable that I'll be lodge-bound. A couple of books, a deck of cards, and the ability to tie a fly or two can make a rainy/sleety day in the lodge a lot more pleasant.

I regard every day I spend in Canada as a treasure to be savored over and over again. But Canada is certainly not the only place where very large pike can be caught. Trophy pike are defined differently in different places. And, depending on where you live, a fifteen-pound pike taken from your local waters may be much more noteworthy than a twenty-five-pounder landed in Canada.

But you can be sure of one thing: the only way any fish gets to be of trophy quality is by being tougher, stronger, and above all, smarter than its peers. In all likelihood, trophy fish have been hooked before. During the course of their long lives, they've seen it all: jerkbaits, soft plastics, live bait, and maybe even a fly or two. To catch a fish of this quality, you'll have to use special tactics and methods.

# CATCHING A TROPHY PIKE

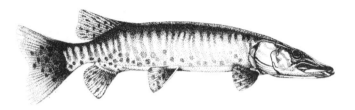

P art of the thrill of fishing for pike lies in the sheer size of the fish. A four-pound trout is bragging material. A six-pound bass will be the subject of many stories. But a pike in the four- to six-pound size range, while terrific sport, is simply a "hammer handle," not worthy of much more than a passing glance before it is returned to the water with a strong admonition to hurry up and grow. No, pike must get much larger to be "big."

When pike do get big, they're just as exciting to catch as you think they will be, probably more. Better still, there are big pike living where you might not expect them. If you take a look at the appendix in the back of this book, you'll discover that pike routinely grow to impressive sizes, even in localities that are not known as top-quality pike fisheries.

I remember my first big northern clearly. Some friends and I went to a favorite lake for early season trout. The ice had been off the water for only about two weeks, and the air was still crisp. I broke what is now a cardinal rule for me and left my nine-weight rod at home. Finding the trout fishing slow, we moved to a shallow bay, thinking that we might pick up a pike or two. The four of us spread out in the shallows, and in short order we began to take an occasional lean and feisty three- to four-pound pike. Clearly, we were catching young, eager males that had arrived on the spawning grounds before the larger, egg-laden females. The day wore on and the waters warmed, and we continued to catch the little males on our light rods. On trout tackle, they were great fun.

Suddenly one of my companions gestured wildly. I looked in the direction of his shaking finger. Long, sleek, and deadly, three big females swam out of the murk. Like three World War I Zeppelins, they ghosted toward us in an arrowhead formation. Each of those fish weighed over twenty pounds.

We were all experienced pike flyfishermen, and it didn't take long for us to begin casting. We threw floaters and divers. We tried a variety of retrieves, but nothing worked. We did everything but chum with our own blood. The three monsters cruised slowly around us, completely ignoring our flies. Finally, as if to add insult to injury, they cruised *between* me and my closest companion, within a few feet of our legs, looped around us, and headed back toward the depths. Just as they were getting out of casting range, I made a double-haul cast that should have broken my rod (or me) and plopped a Deceiver about ten feet in front of the last fish.

I crept the fly back as slowly as I could because I wanted to keep the fly in front of her as long as possible and because it looked as though I'd made my last cast to the trio. The Deceiver went deep, and the white feathers began to fade into the gloom. Then, suddenly, they disappeared.

Praying two selfish prayers (one for the fish to be there, the other for my leader to stand the strain), I leaned back on the rod. It was like setting a hook in a parked Greyhound bus. For what seemed like an eternity, but was only seconds, nothing moved. Then the water fifty feet in front of me exploded in spray, and the bus was in gear. The pike and I spent the next fifteen minutes playing a very wet game of tug-of-war. My leader was woefully light, and I handled the big female like she was a crate of eggs. Perhaps because I couldn't horse the fish, she was one of the rare pike that took me into my backing, and she did so three times. Finally she rolled, gasping, at my feet.

I grabbed her with shaking hands and lifted her up so my companions could be properly envious. Once clear of the water, the fly, which had been sawing around in her jaws for fifteen minutes, simply fell out. Almost as if she knew what had happened, the tough old lady gave one frantic, triumphant wriggle, slipped out of my hands, and was free.

I have worked for years on my companions of that day to get them to accept the fact that what I accomplished was an especially graceful and rapid release, a technique that they would do well to emulate. To date, they haven't bought it. Frankly, I don't think the pike would buy it either. I hope you'll have better luck handling your first big pike.

If cost is no object, Canada is the best place to hunt a trophy. *B. Snellgrove.*

In any case, after you catch a few pike it's only natural to want to start stalking real lunkers. In your pursuit of a trophy pike, the first thing you'll have to decide is what makes a pike a trophy. A trophy can mean different things in different places. If you're fishing in Utah, for example, the pursuit of thirty-pound pike is likely to be a pretty frustrating endeavor. But a twelve-pound pike may be a very respectable fish and may be just as tough to catch as a Canadian pike of twice that size. In Minnesota and Canada, on the other hand, a twelve-pounder is often referred to as "shore lunch."

For the purposes of this chapter, we'll assume that you're going to fish water wherein you have a reasonable chance of finding a genuinely large pike, a fish over forty inches long. If you are dead-level, cost-is-no-object serious about making a try for a fish of this caliber, Canada is the place where your odds of catching one are the best.

During my last trip to Canada, I landed forty-three "over-forty" fish in a seven-day period. The largest fish I took weighed just over thirty pounds. I don't know of any place in the states where pike of this size can be caught in such numbers. But Canadian trips are expensive, time-consuming, and may not fit the needs of other family members. Don't despair. The odds are high that you can also stalk large pike effectively in your local waters. The tactics that follow should make this quest somewhat simpler.

### Catching a Trophy

The most effective tactic for taking trophy pike is probably the most difficult for the average fisherman to put into practice. Simply stated, if you want to catch a trophy, you have to go fishing a lot. It's been my experience that you just have to spend many hours and catch a lot of fish to finally land the monster that (in replica!) will wind up in your den. After you factor in your increasing skill, the quality of the water you're fishing, and a generous serving of sheer luck, catching a trophy fish is, to some extent, still a numbers game.

Although we've all seen pictures in newspapers of the six-year-old kid who, on his first-ever fishing trip, caught a huge fish on a bent pin and a stale potato chip, let's remember that the reason he made the paper was because the occurrence itself was unusual (and the kid was cute). In all likelihood, dumb luck and youthful innocence won't work for you. I would love to tell you how surprised I was to take my world record tiger, but it just wouldn't be true. I took the fish from a municipal reservoir that is very close to my home; I fish the place over a hundred times a year.

I think a description of what went into my efforts to acquire a world record might be instructive. A few years ago, I made one of those arbitrary, capricious decisions for which fishermen are famous: I decided to use only fly tackle and light leaders for tigers. On my seventh cast during my first trip after making this decision, I hooked (and lost after a heartbreaking, twenty-minute battle) a very large tiger. For one shining moment, I thought that I had it made. I didn't know it at the time, but that tiger was my bent-pin-and-potato-chip fish, and I had, for the time being, exhausted my personal share of innocence and dumb luck. Fishing was slow, very slow. I had much to learn.

I spent lots of time on the water watching the fish, following their movements during the day, and watching their hunting and stalking behavior. After a time, I was able to understand how the behavior of the trophy fish I was after—in my lake—differed from the behavior of the run-of-the-mill tiger population. This led me to try different presentations and more lifelike imitations of the forage that was available. In my case, this meant finding a better way to imitate the spot-tailed shiner, which is the predominant forage fish in the lake. After some false starts, I finally made some modifications to a Dan Blanton tarpon pattern that seemed to make the difference. In the next year, I lost six fish over twenty pounds in that same lake. I also nearly lost my mind.

During the next spring, I caught a ton of tigers. They were mostly small fish, with the largest just over three feet long. As the season wore on, larger tigers began to come into the shallows to hunt. As I saw more of these large fish, I experienced more follows, nips, and bumps from the fickle tigers. The three trips prior to catching my record fish were all successful trips. In fact, on the last of these trips, I took nine tigers in one day, and that remains as my best day ever for tiger fishing. And on the evening of that day, a really large tiger made a strong pass at my fly, only to have me jerk it away at the last minute. Pike fever.

By the time I was due to land a record fish, I knew it. I had done my homework and I knew what the fish were taking, where they were holding, and when they were feeding. So, while I was very pleased to catch the fish, I wasn't at all surprised. I worked my tail off for that fish.

## Doing the Homework

The earlier chapters of this book should have left you with the impression that it's no great trick to catch pike on fly tackle. That is as it should be, because with a moderate amount of effort on your part, I'm confident that you will catch pike. On the other hand, catching a trophy pike is just as difficult as catching a trophy trout, bass, or tarpon. You will have to work as hard for your trophy pike as you would for any other trophy-sized fish.

No matter when or where you pursue trophy pike, it's important to remember that really large fish—of any species—are never very numerous. The odds are heavily stacked against any pike reaching trophy size, and the ones that do have learned a trick or two during their long lives. Since jobs, family, and unavailability of quality water can all make it difficult for you to fish as often as I do, what can you do to maximize your odds of finding a trophy and catching it?

When bank robber Willie Sutton was asked why he held up banks, he is reputed to have looked at his interrogator in surprise and said, "Because that's where they keep all the money." Taking a page from Willie's book, my first suggestion would be to make sure you fish where the big fish are. That's what the appendix in the back of this book is for, to allow you to determine where the best pike waters are close to you. Unfortunately for some anglers, this will translate into long trips, but I think that most aspiring pike flyfishermen will be pleased to find that there are good pike waters within a reasonable drive from home.

Using the appendix as a starting point, follow up by talking with state game officials and tackle shop operators in the area you intend to fish. In some states, careful records are kept of where record fish were taken. A little time spent on this kind of research can increase your chances of success.

Once you've chosen your water, stick to it. If the fish are there, it remains for you to figure out where they're holding at particular times of the year. If you skip around to different waters, you may find it difficult to develop the specific local knowledge needed to take a genuine trophy.

Next, streamline your efforts to acquire the knowledge of the water you'll need to fish it most effectively. If you can't fish the water a hundred times a year, you can at least benefit from the experience of someone who does. Once again, talking to local fish and game officials, tackle shop operators, and local anglers can help significantly. If you're really serious about pursuing a trophy-size pike, I would recommend making at least one trip with a guide—a guide who specializes in fishing for pike on your water.

The guide will probably not specialize in guiding flyfishermen, but that's fine. You already know about tactics and strategies that will take pike, and you also know, in a general way, where pike can be found at various times of the year. What you don't know is where the very best pike areas are in your lake. You can certainly acquire this information yourself, if you have the time to do so. But a day spent on the water with a guide, provided that you ask the right questions, can eliminate

A local guide can help you locate the best trophy waters. *B. Snellgrove.*

unlikely water from consideration, which will leave you free to concentrate on prime pike areas.

Before you commit to a guide, let him know what you want to do; you want to spend a day getting an overview of productive pike areas. I can't speak for other guides, but when I guide a party I always assume that part of my job is to function as a mentor, to give my customers the tools they need to be better fishermen whether I'm with them or not. I don't keep secrets. Hopefully, you'll be able to connect with a "teaching guide" as well.

The final thing you can do to maximize your odds of taking a trophy fish is to concentrate your efforts during the most productive times of the year. Since every trophy pike will be a female, this means fishing when you have the best chance of reaching hungry females with fly tackle. There are three "best times" for this.

## Pre-spawn Trophies

For some anglers, this first "best time" will be unavailable, because pre-spawn activity can occur while ice is still present in the shallows. But for anglers who live in areas where the ice melts early in the spring, it is the first time and probably the second-best time overall that the angler has a reasonable opportunity to land a trophy-size pike.

From the chapter on spring fishing, you already know what's going on. As the water warms, pike move into the shallows where they will spawn. Prior to spawning, pike feed heavily to build up an energy reserve to carry them through the spawning season proper, during which they feed lightly, if at all. If you're on the water as soon as it's free of ice, the odds are very good that you'll be able to take advantage of the fine pre spawn fishing.

In all likelihood, you'll catch many small pike. Since small male pike arrive in spawning areas first. Although you can have a ball with these feisty little fellows, we're after a trophy and that means a large female. I admit that it may be tough to do when you're catching fish, but I recommend leaving the action in the shallows and moving out to the first drop-off. Very often, this is where the females are waiting until the shallows are consistently warm enough to provide good incubation for their eggs.

When fishing for these waiting females, presentation is the key. The eager males in the shallows are aggressive and will hit virtually anything. The larger females are, for all intents and purposes, a different fish. They're full of eggs, and the water temperature at the drop-off is likely to be in the high thirties, keeping them sluggish. They are basically in a holding pattern, and therefore, they're after an easy meal. Big flies and slow retrieves at depth are the order of the day.

Timing is also important. Sunny days mean warming water, and this in turn means that the females may begin nosing their way into shallower areas. I've found that fishing in the heat of the day, between 11:00 A.M. and 2:00 P.M., is most productive at this time of the year.

If the water is clear, I recommend using flies in black, white, or combinations thereof. You should also carry some brighter flies, which will allow you to fish mud lines effectively.

As with everything else in the world, there is a tradeoff here. If you stay in the shallows, you'll catch lots of little males and juvenile females, and the action is likely to be fast and furious. If you elect to leave the shallows and work deeper waters for bigger fish, you will almost certainly catch fewer fish. The size of the ones you do catch will usually make up for their relative scarcity. Remember that the large fish you catch will all be females that have yet to spawn. Handle them carefully and return them to the water as soon as you can.

### Post-spawn Trophies

I've said it before, and I'll say it again: the post-spawn season is absolutely the best time to catch pike. It follows that it is also your best shot at a trophy fish. The pike are still in the shallows, which means that large numbers of fish are present in a relatively small area. Due to the rigors of the spawn, they are also hungry and more eager to strike. Pike will remain in the shallows for several weeks after mating and will feed heavily to replace the body mass they've lost during spawning. Aquatic insects are becoming active in the shallows, which in turn brings forage fish in close to shore. Spring breezes regularly stir up the water, creating mud lines that, as we've seen before, are the equivalent of a cafeteria for hungry pike.

Unfortunately, the bigger a pike gets, the more it seems to prefer cold water. Therefore, the really large fish will be the first ones to leave the shallows. This is when using a guide's services can help you. Based on his years of experience on the water, he should be able to provide you with some general guidelines that will help you determine when the pike are done spawning and approximately when the larger fish will begin moving toward cooler water. However, there is no substitute for being a regular visitor to your targeted waters and monitoring the situation yourself.

One of the nice things about this time of year is that any pike fly seems to work. Poppers, divers, Deceivers, and large streamers all take fish. High-speed retrieves are in order, which means you'll cast more often and cover more water during the course of a day. Evenings, when reduced light levels provide additional cover for cruising pike, can also be very productive.

There is only one downside to this scenario. Since both sexes of pike are hungry and since males and juvenile females far out-number trophy-sized females, you may spend an inordinate amount of time catching and releasing smaller fish. As I mentioned above, the pursuit of a trophy pike is to some extent a numbers game, and if you want to catch a big pike, you may find that you will just have to pay your dues by winnowing through a number of smaller fish.

There are two partial cures that you may wish to try for the "problem" of too many small fish. The first is to fish larger flies, 3/0 or bigger, seven inches long or longer. This will keep the real midgets away from your fly.

The other cure relies on the male pike's instinct for self-preservation. During the spawn, an eighteen-inch male may live in what passes for domestic bliss with a forty-inch female; but after the spawn, he moves from the admirable category of "husband" to the much less enviable one of "dinner." So, if the fish you're catching are consistently small, move. The smaller pike (the smart ones, anyway) will, if there is room for them to do so, avoid larger hungry pike. Furthermore, it has been my experience that really large pike tend to be loners. Leaving a productive spot will take real will power on your part, but it can pay off in big fish. Moving just a hundred yards can produce dramatically larger pike.

I put this strategy to good use during a recent trip to Canada. We'd pull into a bay, catch a few fish, and if we didn't like the way the sizes were running, we'd move a couple of hundred yards and try again. On one occasion this paid off in the form of a thirty-pounder. Moving again, we snared two fish of over twenty pounds. Other smaller pike were also present, but not in the quantities that we'd found elsewhere.

**Fall Trophies**

With the onset of fall and before turnover, cooling waters will once again lure large pike into shallower water than where they spend the summer. Since they don't need to find special spawning areas, they'll be more scattered than they were in the spring, and large pike will be found in deeper water (five to twelve feet) than in spring. The scattering of the fish means that large fish will be harder to find; you'll have to cover more water. The good news is that big pike will use the opportunity provided by cooler waters to feed heavily in preparation for the winter. Small pike feed too, but since they've been in shallower water all season long and have been able to feed regularly on forage fish there, they're not driven by the same sense of urgency as are trophy-sized pike.

Boats are very helpful at this time of year because they enable you to cover more water. And because pike are holding in deeper water than they did in the spring, wading may not be practical. If you do use a boat, I've found that anchoring over drop-offs and other structure and then casting into the shallows is an effective technique. It allows me to swim the fly from the shallows out into the structure where the pike are likely to be holding. You should fish the usual fall areas. Don't forget to pay another visit to spring spawning areas. If there is a drop-off reasonably close to them, pike may hold there as well.

You must remember at this time of the year to give your fly time to sink to productive eight- to twelve-foot depths. Most anglers don't wait long enough. Pike will generally hit Bunny Bugs as they sink, and divers as they begin floating toward the surface. Since the water is often clear at this time of the year, my favorite colors for flies are, of course, black patterns and white patterns. Olives and grays can also be good producers.

Slowing your retrieve is crucial. I retrieve, and then I pause—and pause—and pause. Fall strikes tend to be more subtle and they often occur during the pause. The slow-strip lesson was firmly driven home to me several years ago. I had taken a couple of clients to a local lake for some fall trout fishing. By the time we arrived at the lake, the weather wasn't just marginal, it was grim. My customers asked for a rain check, and left to my own devices, I decided to fool around for pike. I started fishing a rocky point that jutted out into a bay. Contrary to my usual procedure, I walked as far out on the point as I could and worked my way back in toward shore.

I spent about an hour-and-a-half covering both sides of the point, casting into about eight feet of water, and caught nothing. I switched flies, tried various retrieves, and when I reached the shallows, switched to a sinking line and a Bunny Bug and began working my way back out along the point again. After another couple of hours of equally unsuccessful fishing, I decided it was time to change flies. I left my Bunny Bug in the water and, placing my rod under my arm, rummaged through my vest for another fly.

After several minutes, I finally selected my next fly. Then I casually began stripping in line so I could tie on the new fly. My first strip was a disappointment; nothing moved. Figuring I was hooked on a rock, I gave the rod a swift jerk, hoping to bounce my fly loose. That's when the "rock" pulled back, hard. Fifteen minutes later I was surprised to find myself holding the biggest pike I've ever taken in Colorado, a forty-three inch, twenty-three pound female.

It's worth remembering that the twenty-three pound pike was my only catch that day and that it took me about four-and-a-half hours of steady casting to catch her. And then I caught her by accident! Welcome to fall trophy fishing. Although this was certainly a trophy-sized fish, I'm proud to say that I didn't kill her. Yet she hangs in my home, and I brag about her regularly. No, this is not as impossible as you might think.

## Trophy Mounts

A big pike hanging on the wall of a flyfisherman's den is an impressive sight. A mounted pike is a long, deadly, torpedo-shaped monster with great big teeth prominently displayed at the business end of the fish. Any fisherman fortunate enough to be able to display such a trophy must have risked his life (or at least his fingers) during the battle that resulted in the capture of the fish. And if he didn't, he can certainly tell people he did.

Before I'm accused of practicing something other than what I preach, I think I should explain how I reconcile my firm belief in catch-and-release fishing with my all-too-human desire to have some bragging material on display. I'm proud of the three trophy-sized pike on my walls at home, but I'm even prouder that I left the fish themselves alive and swimming and that other fishermen will have a chance to experience the same thrill that I did when I caught them.

That's because all of my pike mounts are fiberglass replicas. They're castings made from molds taken from appropriately sized living pike, and they are monuments to the art of the taxidermist. There are some real advantages to buying a fiberglass mount. The first one is obvious: I don't have to kill a trophy fish. If game fish are a valuable resource, trophy fish are pure gold.

The other advantages are more subtle. A conventional mount, made from the skin of the fish you take, is not a durable item. We don't make hiking boots from pike skin for good reason. As years go by, a beautiful conventional mount can deteriorate substantially. Fiberglass replica mounts last forever.

In addition, during the conventional mounting process, color is leached from the fish. All fish mounts, fiberglass or natural, are painted by the taxidermist. Therefore, the accuracy of the mount in terms of coloration is a function of the skill of the taxidermist, not a function of how the fish is mounted. If you select a good taxidermist and if you provide him with good photos of your fish, there is no reason why your fiberglass mount can't be a nearly exact duplicate of your fish. Individual peculiarities in coloring, a notched fin, and even battle scars can be accurately replicated. My mounts are nearly indistinguishable from the real pike I caught.

Finally, if you order a conventional mount, you wind up with a mounted fish that you can proudly display in your home or office—but not both. By using fiberglass mounts and by dipping deeper into your checkbook, it's possible to have duplicate mounts created. Now you can brag at home and at work!

Fiberglass mounts are a bit more expensive, but I think that their durability and the fact that you don't need to kill a trophy fish more than make up for the additional cost. I hope you'll agree.

To have a replica mount made, the first thing you need is a good camera. Self-developing films and Instamatic negatives won't provide the detail and color accuracy you're after. A 35mm camera is a must. The second thing that you need is a way to safely, gently measure the fish. Steel measuring tapes can wound a thrashing pike. I recommend a forty-eight-inch cloth tape like those used by tailors. An assistant is also very, very helpful. The object of the game is to acquire the data you need quickly and get your fish back in the water as soon as possible, and an assistant makes this much easier.

Assuming that you've been fortunate enough to land a large pike, get that camera working! If you can, display the fish so that the sun strikes it. At a minimum, get a photo of the entire fish. If you can crank the film through fast enough, a series of close-ups over the length of the fish will also be helpful. In the heat of the moment, you may not notice individual markings and scars that make your fish unique, but the close-ups will help your taxidermist duplicate your fish more accurately. If you're using a camera with adjustable settings, you may also wish to bracket your exposures, using a couple of settings above and below that recommended by your meter to make sure you get good pictures. You're only going to get one chance!

Once the photos are taken, use your tape to determine the length of the fish; then measure the fish's girth at a couple of points and record where you measured them. For example, you might wish to record girth at the pectoral fins, at the vent, and at a point midway between. This will enable the taxidermist to select a mold that accurately matches your fish.

Finally, get that fish back in the water! I'm sure you're aware this does not mean simply chucking her back in the lake. Supporting the fish carefully, place it gently in the water and "swim" it forward to get water moving through its gills. When the pike has recovered, it will simply swim out of your hands.

With all this in mind, you now have the most difficult task of all.

Having a friend help measure your trophy gets the fish quickly back in the water. *B. Snellgrove.*

You must choose a taxidermist. Outdoor shows are a great place to see taxidermists' work. The folks at your neighborhood fly shop may also have suggestions for you. In either event, when you examine a particular taxidermist's work, ask if it's possible to see the photos from which the fiberglass replicas he's showing you were made. After all, you want the fellow to replicate *your* fish, not just *a* fish, and comparing the finished product with the photos will give you an idea of how good the taxidermist really is. You'll also want to make sure that he has a mold that is large enough to accurately model your fish. If he has to buy or rent one, your costs may increase significantly.

After you've selected a taxidermist, take some time to go over your photos with him. As we all know, colors are not always accurately reproduced on film. The photos, for example, may show your fish as having brick-red fins when they were actually a vivid blood-red. Take some time to explain this sort of thing to the taxidermist; it will help him do a better job.

### The Record Fish

Many fly rod world record slots for pike are vacant, particularly in the case of tigers. Many state records may also be available to the pike flyfisherman. If you fish a lot, if you fish at times when the odds are in your favor, if you get to know your local waters well enough to know where the big pike are likely to be holding and when they are likely to be there, there is a chance that you will, on one great day, land a record pike.

The first thing you'll have to do is decide how badly you want your name in the record books. In the case of all world record fish and most state record fish, you'll have to kill the fish. I've caught one world record fish (a sixteen-pound tiger muskie that is the current National Fresh Water Fishing Hall of Fame fly rod record in the six-pound leader class). I am a working guide, and speaking frankly, being a world record holder adds a great deal of credibility to my guiding endeavors. I killed that fish, but not without mixed feelings. In the final analysis, only you can decide what to do if you're fortunate enough to catch a record fish.

If you decide to keep the fish, the next thing you must do is to make sure that the fish didn't die in vain. Immediately separate the leader and fly from the line and store them carefully. Both of the organizations that keep world records require that you submit a sample of the leader you used to catch the fish.

Naturally, you will also want to have the fish photographed. Make sure you get the name and address of the photographer or of a person who will witness you photographing the fish. The name and address is important, because virtually everyone connected with your fish from this point on will have to submit affidavits testifying to your accomplishment.

Next, you'll have to weigh the fish. This formal weighing can only be performed on a "certified scale." This is a scale that has been certified for use in trade (e.g., scales in supermarkets and delis). This is of crucial importance, and it is where many, many potential records simply disappear. In all likelihood, the scale at the marina or the scale in the kitchen of the bar you always stop at on your way home is not a certified scale. The little scale that has been rattling around in your tackle box for years is certainly not a certified scale. Once again, you'll want to record the name and address of the person who weighs the fish for you. If possible, have a third person witness the weighing and record his or her name and address as well. Make sure you get the fish on a scale as soon as possible, because your pike will begin losing body fluids almost immediately after death.

Then you will make a formal application for a record to the fish and game agency in the state where you caught the fish. This procedure will vary from state to state. If you've been really lucky, you will also be in a position to apply to the International Game Fish Association and/or the National Fresh Water Fishing Hall of Fame for a world record. Upon receipt of your application, they'll send you the requisite affidavits, ask you to submit a sample of your leader for testing, and ask you to provide proof that your fish was weighed on a certified scale. Of course, they will also want photos of your catch.

Handling all this red tape properly is very important. Recently, a muskie that held the world record for over forty years was disallowed because of perceived irregularities in the weighing process.

Is dealing with all of this worth it? You bet it is! A world record fish really is a once-in-a-lifetime achievement that you will treasure forever.

# NINE

# TIGER, TIGER, BURNING BRIGHT

Until recently, the pike a flyfisher was most likely to find on the end of his or her leader was a northern pike. Northern pike are a hardy, prolific fish, and they live naturally or have been successfully introduced in lakes across the United States. Muskies, on the other hand, are more finicky about where they live, and no matter where they live, they do not reproduce as successfully as northerns do. Tiger muskies, the sterile hybrid of northerns and muskies, occur naturally but in such small numbers that in the past they were rarely taken. But the situation with tigers is beginning to change.

Although most anglers and state game agencies now recognize that having balanced populations of predator and prey fish in lakes and rivers translates into better fishing overall, there is still an understandable reluctance on the part of fishery managers to introduce a predator species like the northern pike into quality fishing areas. There are fears that such stocking programs might be a bit too successful, with northerns reproducing too well. The tiger muskie, which grows fast, eats voraciously, and cannot reproduce, answers the need for a large, trophy-quality predator that will not overrun existing fisheries. For this reason, tigers are being stocked in ever-increasing numbers in many states.

Although a tiger muskie exhibits traits common to both northerns and muskies, it seems that tigers have inherited more traits from the muskie side of the family. Like muskies, tigers can be "a fish of a thousand casts" and as a rule are much tougher to catch than northerns, unless you're like my son, Mike, who as a four-year-old nailed a sixteen-pound tiger on his first cast with his new discount-house spincast rig. Mike's reel jammed seconds after he hooked the fish, and he had to land his tiger by holding his rod firmly and walking slowly away from the lake. Later, when I opened up the reel to see what had gone wrong, I poured the fused and broken remnants of the reel's mechanism out into my hand. Tigers are tough!

When flyfishing for tigers, you need to think in terms of warmer water temperatures. This works out well, because as shallow water temperatures reach the high sixties and northerns are retreating to deeper, cooler waters, tigers begin to feed most actively in the shallows.

A pike as long as the angler is tall. Barry, Mike, and a sixteen-pound, first-cast tiger. *S. Reynolds.*

In many parts of the country, this translates into fine tiger fishing in July and August and serves to extend the pike season by two months.

Like its parents, the tiger comes into the shallows as the waters warm in the spring, typically when the water reaches the low to mid-fifties. Since tigers don't spawn, their feeding behavior is "business as usual" rather than the frenzied feeding of pre- and post-spawn northerns and muskies. Some experts consider this behavior to be a sort of false spawn, while others believe that tigers come into the shallows because that's where most of the forage fish are in the spring. I tend to favor the latter hypothesis because, although I've seen many tigers cruising the shallows in the spring, I've never seen them seek out what I would call genuine pike spawning areas in preference to other shallow areas.

### Tiger Behavior

I've made much of the voracious and aggressive nature of northerns. It's not at all uncommon to catch a northern that still has the tail of its last meal protruding from its mouth. Whether you call it greed, aggressiveness, or sheer bad temper, it's fairly clear that the state of a northern's belly has comparatively little to do with its willingness to hit your fly.

Tigers are much different. Because the fish is a relative newcomer in Colorado, many of our tigers wind up in the hands of taxidermists. Over the past few years, I've asked several local taxidermists to make a note of the stomach contents of the tigers they receive for mounting. Out of thirty tigers, twenty-four had empty stomachs. This is not much of a sample, and it is obviously skewed toward larger, trophy-quality fish. It does, however, make me believe that tigers aren't typically a "gorging" fish and that the tigers caught by anglers are likely to be hungry fish, rather than aggressive fish who were induced to strike by a tantalizing or irritating fly.

This characteristic alone will reduce your odds of success with tigers. On the other hand, a hungry tiger can be a very aggressive fish, indeed. Several years ago, I had a very pleasant day on a nearby reservoir. I wasn't catching any large tigers, but I was taking a twenty-four-inch hammer handle every forty-five minutes or so, and that kind of action for tigers is more than sufficient to hold my interest. I hooked another little tiger, played it for a bit, and then brought it in to the side of my boat so I could release the fish. I did a snake grab on the little fellow and was in the process of removing the fly from its jaw when the water literally exploded in my face. When my vision cleared, I noticed that I was missing something—one two-foot tiger. I also noticed that my line was moving.

I let my gaze travel out along the line, and at the end of it discovered at least forty inches of tiger muskie that had my little tiger crossways in its jaws. The big tiger seemed to be quite pleased with itself. The little tiger expressed no opinion.

I was then presented with a rather interesting ethical dilemma. The regulations at the lake allowed fishing with artificial flies and lures only. The little tiger (known hereafter as Tiger A) had taken a fly. The larger tiger (Tiger B) had clearly taken a living fish, but the fish it took was just as clearly not bait—or at least it hadn't started out that way. I wondered if I should:

- jerk Tiger A from the jaws of Tiger B; or
- try to inadvertently catch Tiger B (a fine, forty-inch fish that had to weigh over twenty pounds), throwing myself on the mercy of the local game warden if necessary.

Things became more interesting when that same game warden quietly drifted his boat up to mine and asked how things were going. I must confess that I didn't have much of an answer. Just then, Tiger B opened its mouth as though it were going to make matters clear to both the warden and to me. At that point, Tiger A seemed to have heard its mother calling, because it immediately departed the scene at a high rate of speed. Although Tiger B tried to convince Tiger A to stay awhile, it was unsuccessful. Smarting from this case of social rejection, Tiger B promptly left, as well. Since Tiger A was still attached to my line, it remained for me to hoist this very bewildered fish from the lake a couple of minutes later.

"Nice little fish," commented the warden. "It looks like something's been chewing on him, doesn't it?"

Tiger B was obviously one very hungry, aggressive tiger, and its behavior was not the norm. In general, I've found tigers to be much more spooky than northerns. Noisy, sloppy approaches cause them to quickly leave the area, most likely before you even catch a glimpse of them. When fishing for northerns, it's common to go back and successfully catch a fish that has followed or has struck at and missed your fly. Not so with tigers. If they miss your fly, they're usually gone.

Tigers can exhibit another behavior that I find to be particularly perplexing. I've seen tigers swimming around with their heads completely out of the water, for all the world like a water snake. Are they looking for prey? Are they looking for me? Are they looking for other predators? Maybe they're working on their tans! I have no idea, but this behavior emphasizes the fact that tigers are different from other pike.

Unlike either of its parents, a tiger will often reward the flyfisherman who's caught one with a fine display of acrobatics. Pound for pound, I think that tigers have more stamina than northerns. They also regularly pull more tricks than do northerns. In addition to leaping, tigers dive, sulk, headshake, and roll in frantic efforts to rid themselves of the angler's fly.

Like fishing for the much-less-common muskellunge, tiger fishing requires you to be willing to make those thousand casts if you have to. It requires you to fish in a stealthy and systematic fashion. Most of all, it demands that you be innovative enough to change tactics to

Tigers regularly pull more tricks than northerns—leaping, diving, and rolling. *B. Reynolds.*

meet the demands of this capricious fish. In my opinion, any tiger taken on a fly rod is a trophy of sorts.

## Tiger Tactics

When I go after tigers, I prefer to fish a small lake. I can hit most of a small lake's prime tiger areas in a one-day outing. With luck, I'll be able to hit some of them several times. In addition, small lakes are more likely to be fishing-only lakes. While northerns are often tolerant of roaring ski-boats and jet-skis, tigers are more skittish. But the most significant attribute of a smaller lake is that I can quickly discover most of the areas where the tigers are likely to be holding. This is important, because you'll always have to figure out what fly is appealing to the tigers *that* day. This task alone is tough enough without also having to make an extensive search for the fish.

In my experience the peak times for fish for tigers are between 10:00 A.M. and 1:00 P.M. and 6:00 P.M. and sundown, but my tiger days typically begin earlier. Whether wading or boating, my first task is to check all the areas that I know, both from my overall experience with pike and my specific knowledge of a given lake, are favorite tiger spots. It should not surprise you to find that I check downed trees, weed lines, saddles, rocky banks, and other pike hangouts. Normally tigers are loners, but they can congregate in groups when prime habitat is limited. When this occurs, the pike that group together will all be very close to the same size.

At this stage of the game I'm not fishing; rather, I'm running my route to see who's at home. If no one is home, it's usually because they're out hunting. When I find no tigers at their favorite spots, I move to the nearest weed line and fan cast the area on the theory that the tigers are hunting for forage fish in the weeds. The theory holds true often enough for me to continue the practice. I fish both the outside and the inside of weed lines. The inside will be shallower than the outside, and tigers will often combine sunbathing in the warm shallows with hunting forays for crawdads and bait fish. As you check weed lines, mud lines, and other hunting grounds, keep an eye out for fleeing bait fish. Often you'll never see the tiger that is causing all the commotion.

In the case of my record tiger, I saw hundreds of little wakes left by terrified bait fish long before my tiger, accompanied by an even bigger pike, drifted into sight. Like a couple of fighter planes making a strafing run, the two tigers made a quick pass through the school of

The smaller of the two fish charging the fly, this tiger was still a line-class world record. *D. Thornton.*

minnows and then cleverly drifted out to the depths so that the school could form again. When their prey had quieted down, they returned. That was my signal to cast to the pair. Rushing ahead of the other fish, the smaller of the two immediately approached my fly in the purposeful fashion that in my experience meant a "bump." To my surprise, the fish gently inhaled my fly.

For the tiger flyfisherman, the ability to work known holding and hunting areas systematically is crucial. When we fish for northerns, our task is to locate a fish whose naturally aggressive nature make it at least an even bet that it will hit our fly. The situation with tigers is almost precisely the opposite: locating the fish is not nearly as tough as convincing the fish you do find to strike. I think the most effective strategy for tigers consists of maximizing the time spent discovering what the fish are interested in, rather than searching for fish.

Now let me quickly dispel any hopes that you might have that I have any great secrets in this regard. I simply try everything until something works. Depending on my mood, I will start out with a floater or a diver. I try fast retrieves, slow retrieves, surface flies, divers, sinking flies, attractors, and relatively accurate imitations of crawdads or specific forage fish species until I get a positive response. Carrying two rods makes this process much simpler because I'm able to switch easily and quickly between sinking and floating presentations.

All this can be an agonizing process. Sometimes you can do no wrong and sometimes you can't do anything right. Since I began fly-fishing for pike, there have been several occasions in Canada when I've caught over seventy large northern pike in one day. In the United States, I've caught over twenty northerns in a day enough times that I've stopped keeping track. On my very best day for tigers to date, I caught exactly nine fish. On my second-best day, I caught five fish. There have been many, many no-fish days.

## Flies for Tigers

Like northerns, tigers will take both floating and subsurface flies. While tigers hit floating flies as strongly as northerns do, their reaction to a subsurface fly is quite different. Where a northern slams a sinking Bunny Bug, a tiger is more prone to nibble and nip. On many occasions, I've seen tigers firmly bump a subsurface fly with closed jaws. They may be trying to injure the prey, or they may be able to "taste" through the sensory pores in their lower jaws and so bump the fly to see if it's good to eat. They may be just trying to annoy me. Although nine out of ten of these "bumpers" will promptly swim off after nosing the fly, the tenth one will take the fly immediately, further confounding the issue.

Diver-type flies work well for tigers, particularly when used in combination with sink-tip or full-sink lines. With divers, tigers prefer a very slow retrieve. The majority of strikes on a diver come when I've stopped retrieving, and the diver is slowly making its way back to the surface.

A slow retrieve isn't always the answer. When they're hitting streamers, tigers seem to prefer a very rapid retrieve. In fact, sometimes it is physically impossible to retrieve them fast enough to interest a tiger. When this happens, I don't fight it; I tie on a diver. In general, streamers are still very effective for tigers. They sink to depth fast, and rapid retrieves mean that you can cover a lot of water quickly and efficiently. My favorite streamer tactic is to cast over a weed line, let the streamer sink, and then retrieve the fly just over the tops of the weeds.

I tell myself that this mimics a bait fish escaping over the top of weedy cover. I can't testify as to what the tigers think, but I do know that they take streamers retrieved in this fashion pretty regularly.

Size seems to mean little to tigers. At roughly the same time of the year, I've taken tigers on both small trout streamers and seven-inch pike bucktails.

If you demand lots of action from your fishing, if you require your quarry to behave in a predictable, rational fashion, and if you expect success to come to you quickly, the odds are that tiger hunting is not for you. On the other hand, if you enjoy the chase as much as the capture, if you delight in the irrational, unpredictable aspects of the world around us, and if a thousand seems to be a relatively manageable number, then I think you'll enjoy hunting for tigers.

# Pike Tackle and Gear

Most of you will begin your pike fishing with the tackle you already own. There's nothing wrong with this; there's no sense in investing in new gear until you're sure you'll enjoy flyfishing for pike. Over the long term, however, lighter gear is simply not up to the stresses that come with repeated casting of large, heavy flies. Casting these flies on light tackle isn't much fun either. If you're as successful as I hope you'll be in your pursuit of pike, I think you'll eventually decide that an investment in heavier gear is warranted.

This process doesn't have to cost a fortune, although it certainly can. As long as you shop at a reputable fly shop that stocks name-brand equipment and seek the help of a knowledgeable salesperson, it's pretty difficult to buy bad equipment these days.

When appropriate in the paragraphs that follow, I'm going to mention brand names of the equipment I use. This equipment has served me faithfully for season after season of rugged use, but there are many other fine makes of tackle on the market.

## Rods for Pike

For pike fishing, there are three line weights that will serve you well, eight, nine, and ten. As you might expect, there are compromises to be made. An eight-weight rod is a bit light for pike, but it doubles as a fine bass or steelhead rod. If the pike in your neck of the woods don't run to monster sizes or if you plan to do a lot of bass fishing, an eight-weight, nine-foot rod is an excellent choice. A ten-weight rod, on the other hand, is a bit heavy for pike, but it can also do double duty as a salmon or saltwater rod.

While I've used both these rod weights for pike fishing, I've settled on nine-weight, nine- and nine-and-a-half-foot rods as ideal for my purposes. A nine-weight rod is also a good bass rod, particularly if you fish around lots of heavy cover or routinely throw big flies. It's also a perfect size for most steelhead, salmon, and light saltwater flyfishing. Recently, rod makers have made significant advances in design and construction techniques. Today you can purchase multi-piece rods that perform very nearly as well as two-piece rods. If you plan to do a lot of traveling, a three-piece rod or a four-piece pack rod may be just what you need. I've stuck with two-piece rods so far, but I do routinely carry four-piece rods with me as back-up rods when I'm traveling.

When you're shopping for your pike rod, you might want to look for one with a fighting butt, particularly if you fish in weedy areas and are likely to have to horse out a belligerent pike. One commonly available fighting butt is detachable. You carry it in a pocket until you hook a fish, then insert it in the rod. Other rods in these heavier line weights may have the fighting butt permanently attached. Some manufacturers now make fighting butts that telescope out of the butt, so they're out of the way until they're needed.

If you're a trout fisherman, you've probably been waiting for me to embark on a long technical discourse about the kind of action I prefer in my rods and why you should feel the same way about rod action as I do. Prepare to be disappointed. The truth is that in the case of fly rods for heavy line weights, there really is no such thing as "soft" or "slow" rods as trout anglers know them. These rods are intended to throw heavy lines and bulky flies. Because of this, they are all comparatively "fast." That is not to say that some rods aren't faster than others. My suggestion? If you're comparing two rods, purchase the faster one, since this will make casting a sodden Bunny Bug much easier. Because higher-modulus graphite rods are faster than traditional graphite, I recommend you choose from among them.

You should compare pike rods differently than you do trout rods. When you audition a trout rod, the salesperson attaches reel and line and sends you out to the back lot to cast it. That's fine, because most trout flies are, for all intents and purposes, weightless. This is not the case with pike flies. I would suggest that you come to the store equipped with a de-hooked Bunny Bug and a pike leader like the ones you'll use most often. Attach all this to end of the line you'll be using, and then make sure to soak the fly so it's waterlogged and heavy, just as it will be when you use it. This is very important. If you haven't as

Heavy rods with fighting butts are the standard for the demands of pike fishing. *B. Snellgrove.*

yet cast a big pike fly, you won't appreciate how heavy a waterlogged Bunny Bug can be. You can't audition a pike rod effectively unless you cast the fly and leader.

As for my personal preferences, I like the higher-modulus graphite rods and have used a Sage 996 RPL for many years. You should, of course, try out several brands to find the rod that pleases you. Loomis, Orvis, and other companies also make high-modulus graphite rods that are respected in saltwater and steelhead circles. With the help of fly shop personnel and a wet Bunny Bug, you should find the perfect pike rod.

## Reels for Pike

With the increased interest in saltwater, salmon, and steelhead fly-fishing, there are better heavy-duty reels on the market than ever before. You'll have some shopping to do.

Look for a reel that has a strong, smooth, reliable drag. In saltwater reels, rugged drags are built to withstand the long, tearing runs of bonefish and the violent acrobatics of tarpon. Pike are clearly not in this class, but they are capable of repeated thirty- to fifty-foot dashes, and if you don't have a reliable drag, overruns and lost fish will be an inevitable result.

For your purposes, you need a drag that can handle the repeated, very fast runs made by a pike. You're after a drag that releases smoothly in response to those sudden, jerking runs. If you're going to ask your new reel to handle only pike, a simple, smooth drag may work fine for you. On the other hand, if you expect to fish in the saltwater or for salmon or steelhead, I recommend spending the extra dollars to upgrade the drag.

You'll also remember that pike change depth in response to temperature, forcing you to change lines to reach them. For this reason, make sure you can change spools quickly and easily. Some saltwater reels, for example, need to be partially disassembled to change spools, and this is simply too cumbersome for the pike flyfisherman.

I'll leave the issue of backing capacity up to you. The vast majority of pike you catch (even very large ones) will never take you into your backing; but the one that does will make you think you've somehow caught a bonefish by mistake. I like substantial backing capacity for two reasons: first, it is cheap insurance against the pike that decides to show me just how fast and strong she really is. Second, it serves to increase the diameter of the spool, which permits me to retrieve line much faster.

There is a final consideration to take into account. In the nine-weight class, there are really two kinds of reels on the market. One group consists of freshwater reels that are primarily made to be used for salmon, bass, pike, and steelhead. The second group consists of reels that are intended for sustained use in saltwater. These reels feature special alloys, plating, and anodizing that enable them to withstand the corrosive effects of saltwater. As you might expect, they are more expensive and heavier than reels designed for freshwater. If you intend to use your tackle in saltwater any time in the future, buy a reel suitable for that use.

I've been using Ross reels for many years, and they represent a mid-priced reel with all the features you'll require for pike. Other reels for the price-conscious shopper are the Lamson and the Scientific Anglers System II. STH, Orvis, Abel, and several other manufacturers make reels you should also investigate. Some of these reels are simply more money than I'm willing to invest, but reels less expensive than the Ross may not give the years of service it does. Ross makes two models for the freshwater angler, the Ross G-3 (for line weights eight and nine) and G-4 (for weights nine and ten). Like the reels of other well-known makers, they're attractively made and feature fine engineering, reliability, and durability. If a trip to the Keys or Costa Rica is in your future, the Ross saltwater models are the GS-3 and the GS-4. These reels feature tougher drags than the freshwater models, are saltwater resistant, and will hold more backing.

You may find many acceptable reels in your local fly shop. Price and personal taste will help you make your choice.

### Lines for Pike

Today, there are many brands of lines on the market, as well as a bewildering variety of tapers, sink-tip lengths, sink rates, finishes, stiffnesses, and colors. For the pike flyfisherman, working your way through all these choices is important. Having the correct line means being able to cast cumbersome pike flies efficiently and being able to fish at the right depth to reach pike.

Many of the decisions about lines will have to be left to you. Sink-tip length and sink rates depend on the water you'll be fishing and your skill as a fly caster. Your fly shop can help with those choices. There are, however, a few decisions I can help with. For instance, I always buy a weight-forward line because it casts heavy flies so much better. For floating lines, bass-bug tapers, a type of weight-forward line designed to cast bulky flies, work very well for pike flies. I also carry a sink-tip line and a sinking line with weight-forward tapers. If you're not excited about buying two spare spools for your reel, I recommend equipping your reel with a floating, weight-forward line and carrying at least one spare spool with a sinking line so you can handle both surface and subsurface needs.

When you shop for lines, you'll discover that they come in more colors than the folks at Crayola ever thought of. This can be confusing, but it shouldn't be. Choose any color you like. The pike won't care. Early in my pike flyfishing days, I worried about bright colors. I even experimented with darkening the first ten feet of line with markers. It made no difference.

I use Cortland lines because I believe the extra stiffness of the 444SL line improves my casting. You may prefer lines by manufacturers such as Scientific Anglers and Orvis. Other well-known companies include Fenwick, Teeny Lines, Wulff Tapers, and Air-Flo, and new entries are a regular feature of the fly line market.

Whatever line you get, be sure to spend the money necessary to get a good one. There's no worse investment than a cheap line. They cast poorly, coil up in cold weather, and do not wear as well over the years.

## Pike Leaders

Leaders are extremely important to the pike flyfisherman, as they are for trout and bass anglers, but they are very different from leaders for these fish. Trout leaders, for instance, are carefully designed to turn over a dry fly or to allow a nymph to drift in a natural fashion. They're tapered to make delicate presentations and have very fine tippets. Bass leaders are shorter and stouter than trout leaders, but they are still usually tapered, and the teeth of a bass are not a concern in leader construction.

The pike flyfisherman faces different problems, and pike leaders reflect that fact. Big, hairy pike flies will never enter the water with any delicacy; they're just too big and heavy. Even if they did land delicately, it wouldn't matter to the pike. So, there's no need to taper a pike leader, and with the size of pike and pike flies, a fine tippet is out of the question.

Pike do have teeth, and unlike the conical "grabbers" that outfit the jaws of a trout or bass, pike teeth are genuine "slicers" that are quite capable of cutting through most monofilament leaders. To make matters worse, pike don't just grab a fly, they *bite* it. So, pike leaders must be resistant to bite-through, but they should also be relatively inconspicuous and easy enough to work with that you can readily change flies. With all this in mind, there are two basic types of leader systems for pike: straight-mono systems and wire/mono systems.

Straight-mono leaders are less visible than wire/mono systems, and they permit the fly to "swing" more naturally, giving it better

Pike teeth are "slicers" that can cut most monofilament leaders. *B. Snellgrove.*

action. However, pike can cut even a very heavy mono leader, and because the material itself is thicker than wire, it doesn't slice through weeds as well as wire can.

Mono/wire leader systems have been the standard for many years. Even a large pike won't cut through the wire portion of the leader, and when the pike seeks to escape by running through the weeds, the wire does a better job of cutting itself free. On the other hand, wire kinks, and a frantically writhing pike can turn your nice wire shock tippet into something that looks a lot like a Slinky. You'll have to discard the leader at that point. In addition, most brands of wire are impossible to knot in traditional ways, so you must use special techniques to attach the wire shock tippet to the monofilament leader and the fly. However, very recently Orvis has begun selling a special wire that can be knotted, eliminating one of my major complaints.

My own preference is for straight-mono systems as long as only hard-monofilament leader material is used. Mason and Rio make hard monofilament. This material is cranky to use; there's nothing limp or soft about it. It is *hard*, but in my experience it's the only monofilament that stands up to a pike's teeth. In fact, during my last Canada trip, my partner and I landed over four hundred pike using Mason monofilament, and we lost only four fish to "bite-offs." Let's look at these leader systems in more detail.

### Straight-mono Leaders

Day-in and day-out, I think you will be best served by the simplest, most reliable leader system available. In my opinion, twenty-five-pound-test hard monofilament roughly the length of your rod is the best way to go.

When you take the material off the spool, you'll be unimpressed. It's hard and tends to remain in stubborn coils. But its vice is also its virtue; it will withstand the pike's knife-edged teeth. You'll just have to spend more time working the leader though the pads of your leader straightener.

Hard mono has one additional characteristic that, depending on your knot-tying skills, you will or won't like. Because it's so stiff, complex knots are out. I use pre-made braided nylon loops on the ends of all my fly lines, and I've never had one fail. To attach the hard mono to the loop, I use a clinch knot, which trout anglers will recognize as the simplified form of the improved clinch knot. I only make three turns of the tag end around the standing portion of the leader. If you make the improved clinch knot's usual five or six turns, the hard mono won't snug-up firmly. Another knot that will work is the perfection loop, as long as it's carefully tied. The benefit of the perfection loop is, of course, that you can then make a loop-to-loop connection between line and leader, which greatly facilitates changing leaders.

Anglers who are used to tying a leader to a plain monofilament butt section will be tempted to try blood knots or surgeon's knots. I've found them very difficult to tie in hard monofilament. No matter which knot option you choose, make sure you use ample supplies of the "universal lubricant," saliva, on the leader to allow it to slide on itself easily as you snug up the knot.

To attach the fly to the leader, I choose the simplest knot, a clinch knot, again tied with no more than three turns around the leader proper. If you want a bit more action, you may wish to try using a Duncan loop, again limiting the number of loops to about three.

There is one additional trick to using mono leader systems. After you catch a pike, take a moment to pass the last two feet or so of leader across your lips (which are more sensitive than your cold, wet fingers). If you feel roughness, the pike has succeeded in abrading some of the nylon. I take no chances; when I feel a rough spot, I trim the leader and re-attach the fly.

There are two reasons why you might wish to complicate this system: if you want to set a line-class record or if you are plagued by very heavy vegetation. In the case of a line-class record, you must fish with lighter leader, although a shock tippet is permitted. When you're dealing with thick vegetation, you'll find that twenty-five-pound leader doesn't slice through the vegetation as well as thinner twelve- or fifteen-pound material will. Moving to lighter leader may help you bring the pike you catch out of the weeds.

For these setups, I use about eight feet of conventional twelve-pound level leader (or the appropriate line-class test) combined with a twenty-five-pound hard-mono shock tippet two or three feet long. The twelve-pound conventional leader is attached to the line by whatever means you choose. I like loop-to-loop connections. The hard-mono shock tippet is attached to the leader in one of three ways. My first choice is the blood knot. Admittedly, the Mason material makes it tough to tie, but the results are worth it if the knot is tied properly. My second choice is a double surgeon's knot. It ties quickly and reliably and is especially suited to splicing lines of varying diameters. My third choice is to use small, neat perfection loops on the leader and shock tippet to make loop-to-loop connections. The advantage of this system is that you can change shock tippets quickly. The disadvantages are that the joint between the two leader materials is somewhat more visible and may pick up weeds.

### Wire/Mono Leaders

Until the advent of hard-monofilament material, a wire/mono leader system was the system of choice for pike, and many pike fishermen still use them. If you absolutely refuse to run a chance of a pike biting your fly off, consider a wire/mono system.

Store-bought wire/mono leaders are available, and they work fine. They are available in a limited range of lengths and sizes, and they cost a lot more than homemade leaders. If you choose to make your own, I'd recommend combining eight feet of conventional eight- to ten-pound level leader material with a two- or three-foot tippet made from twenty-five-pound plastic-coated, braided wire.

For many years, the Albright knot was the only good way to attach a wire shock tippet to a monofilament leader. It is still a fine knot, but as you change flies during the course of a day's fishing, the wire tippet

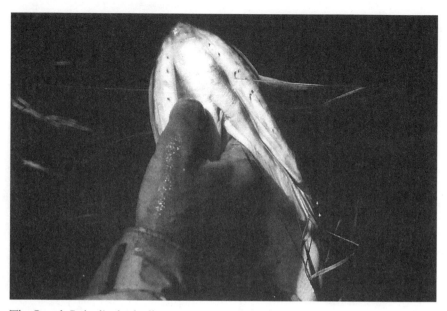

The Leech Lake lip-lock allows you to control a fish that wants to roll away from the snake grab. *B. Snellgrove.*

will get shorter and shorter. Eventually you'll have to switch leaders or tie another Albright knot.

There is a better way. First, tie a neat perfection loop in the end of the mono leader. Next, tie a "melt knot" in the wire. Here's how a melt knot is tied. Form a loop in the wire; then, wrap the short end of the loop around the main portion of the wire six or eight times. The wraps should form a spiral extending about an inch or an inch-and-a-quarter along the leader. Then, flick your Bic and apply heat carefully to the wraps. You want to melt the plastic coating of the leader but not burn it! If you char the plastic, the knot won't work, and you'll have to start over. The first time I saw this knot tied, I couldn't believe that it would work. After using this method for several years, I'm now sold on it. I've never had a melt-knot fail. The loop you've just formed will permit you to make loop-to-loop connections to the leader. I also use this melt-knot method to attach the fly to the wire leader by running the wire through the eye of the fly before forming the loop. Be sure to carry a tool suitable for cutting wire if you use a wire/mono system. Needle-nosed pliers, like those I recommend for removing deeply hooked flies, often have back cutters that work fine for cutting wire.

## Other Accessories

I enjoy wading for pike. There's no better way to cover productive water systematically, and I think a stealthy, careful wader disturbs fish less than a boat does. When wading for pike, neoprene is the only material I would recommend. Spring pike fishing weather can be cold, and you'll want every bit of the insulation that neoprene provides. I wear chest-highs, as much for extra warmth around my torso as for the ability to wade a bit deeper. I also prefer stocking-foot waders, because I can then purchase wading shoes that really fit well. I spend many hours in my waders, and comfort is very important.

In vests, I prefer a shorty, because it permits me to wade deep if I have to. For reasons that will become clear in a moment, I'm more concerned with being able to store rain gear, cameras, and tools than I am with having a lot of pockets for fly boxes, so I look for a vest with big pockets.

Fly boxes are more important to trout anglers because they need to store many kinds of flies in a compact, organized manner. The pike angler's needs are almost precisely the opposite: rarely will you carry more than a dozen different patterns, although you may wish to carry several copies of each pattern. In addition, the flies will be big and easy to manage. In light of these quite different requirements, I have evolved a simple, effective way to store large pike flies in my vest: I put them in Ziploc storage bags.

Before you start laughing, think about this system more carefully. You don't have to worry about crushing delicate hackles, so you can jam a bag of flies in a very small space. Further, the bags are transparent, so you can select flies and keep track of your inventory easily. Finally, the system is certainly cheap enough. There is one disadvantage. Conventional fly boxes are vented to permit used flies to dry. Ziplocs won't allow flies to dry. To avoid mildew, put used flies in a separate bag and at the end of the day empty the bag and allow the flies to dry.

Here's something you won't need. I don't use nets, and I don't recommend them. Pike are long and snaky, and getting one into a net usually involves some folding and coercing of the fish that can only stress the animal and rub off its protective coating. If you really feel that you need some help, I would recommend the use of a cradle. Used like a stretcher, a cradle is held under the water while the pike is guided over it. The cradle is lifted, with the fish comfortably slung within. This is generally a two-person operation. If you positively must have a net, get a net big enough to do the job.

The snake grab allows you to hold the fish, while jaw spreaders make removing the fly easier and safer. *B. Snellgrove.*

## The Snake Grab

If I don't use these aids, what do I do? I grab the pike, in one of two safe and effective fashions. The snake grab is about as easy as it sounds. I simply reach down on the back of the fish and grab the pike where the head meets the body, behind but not in the gills. This allows me to control even very large pike while they're in the water.

The Leech Lake lip-lock may sound more difficult, but it's really quite easy to perform and works well on a pike that persists in rolling away from you. Slide your hand under the pike, below and to the outside of the gill plate. This keeps you from tearing up the pike's gills and also keeps your fingers away from spines on the gills. Keep sliding your hand forward until it stops. You will then have your fingers around the fleshy part of the underside of the mouth (where the "second chin" would be on a human), and you can control the fish easily.

When I say "control the fish," I mean being able to keep the fish still until you can remove your hook from its jaw and get some photos. My preference for a pose is to place my free hand under the rear of the fish and simply lift it from the water far enough that a picture can be taken. Cradle the fish as best you can and get your pictures taken quickly so you don't cause internal injuries that can kill the fish.

When removing the fly (from the fish or from you), the value of barbless hooks is clear. In the majority of cases, I simply pluck the fly from the pike's jaws. Occasionally I'll catch a pike that has managed to take the fly deeply. Because the fly is debarbed, it will still come out easily, if I can get a grip on it. This task will at first glance appear to be an easy one. In all likelihood, the pike will obligingly open its mouth so you can remove the fly. This impression of cooperation is a false one; the pike is opening its mouth so it can bite the hell out of you when you stick your fingers in. This is not hyperbole. Unlike most other freshwater fish, a pike will definitely bite you if it gets a chance. Then it will thrash its heavy body around to make sure that it makes nice, deep wounds.

Needle-nosed pliers at least eight inches long are the answer. I used to have a great pair of stainless steel, extra-long, needle-nosed pliers that cost every bit of thirty bucks. A pike that was tougher than I thought it was swam away with them in its jaws, so a lanyard is also a good idea. Jaw-spreaders also help you get that deeply hooked fly. Although these gadgets are readily available commercially, some fly-fishermen make their own from wire. Basically, you bend up a big safety pin (about seven inches long) with hooks on the end of the long arms. This affair is placed in the jaws of the pike, and the spring in the wire holds the jaws open so you can snake your pliers in to get the fly.

For me, there is simply nothing better than sight fishing for big pike, and you absolutely must have polarized sunglasses to do this efficiently. I've been disappointed every time I've purchased low-cost sunglasses, so I buy the best polarized glasses I can afford. As a final note, the sight of anyone flyfishing without eye protection makes my blood run cold. Pike flyfishermen throw huge flies that invite mistakes in casting. And, if you flyfish for pike from a boat, two rods and two flies in close proximity increase the chances of an accident. Always, always wear eye protection!

Those huge flies pike anglers use are quite different from what you're probably used to. But they're just as vital as the gear I've described in this chapter. A dozen or so of my favorites are covered in the next chapter.

# FAVORITE PIKE FLIES

The fly patterns included in this chapter are ones that I use routinely, and they've all produced a lot of fish for me. Some of them will be suitable for those starting out with lighter rods, while others really require the use of heavier gear. Although I've described how I usually present and retrieve the fly, this should not, of course, prevent you from experimenting with other methods.

Most of these flies can easily be tied by a moderately skilled fly tier. However, a couple of them are quite taxing, and unless you enjoy the challenge of tying a difficult fly, I recommend buying these patterns. In addition, although the patterns give my favorite color for each fly, I urge you to find the colors that work best for you in your local waters. Finally, although I've included patterns for the flies, I have not included specific tying instructions, since this book is not intended to be a fly-tying manual.

## BUNNY BUG

If you don't know what I'm going to say about this fly, then you haven't been paying attention. By virtue of the ease with which this fly is tied, the economy of the materials used, its durability, and—most importantly—its effectiveness, the Bunny Bug gets my vote as the best overall fly for pike. Spring, summer, and fall, pike belt Bunnies with abandon, but even large pike have a tough time mangling the rabbit skin with which the fly is made. Thanks to the popularity of Zonker-type streamers, rabbit strips are now available in a bewildering variety of colors that will permit the fly tier to match the colors of bait fish, leeches, and crawdads.

Bunny Bug. *J. Berryman.*

Depending on the time of year, my retrieves will vary from halt-ing, hesitant strips that cause the fly to "breathe" seductively to rapid, yard-long strips that compress the fur and make the fly look very much like a fleeing bait fish. Floating lines and rapid retrieves allow me to fish Bunnies in fairly shallow water, while sinking lines and slower retrieves permit me to go deep for trophies.

The only disadvantage to the Bunny Bug is that, when wet, it weighs about as much as a small brookie, or maybe a medium brookie. Casting Bunnies on light rods can be, well, "thrilling." But if you are equipped with proper tackle, the Bunny Bug is as important to pike fishing as the Gold-Ribbed Hare's Ear and the Adams are to trout fishing, and you should carry your Bunny Bugs in the vest pocket next to your heart.

**Materials for the Bunny Bug**

| | |
|---|---|
| *Hook:* | Saltwater or salmon wet fly, e.g., Mustad #34007 or Tiemco TMC 811S, size 3/0 |
| *Weed Guard:* | 25-pound hard mono |
| *Thread:* | Black |
| *Tail:* | Black rabbit strip, 4″ long, topped with several strands of black Krystal Flash, just shorter than tail |
| *Butt:* | Orange (or other bright color) marabou |
| *Body:* | Black rabbit strip 6″ long, palmered to ¼″ of eye |

*Head:* Black thread, lacquered
*Eyes:* Applied with Faber-Castell Uni-Point Paint Markers

Lefty's Deceiver  *J. Berryman.*

## LEFTY'S DECEIVER

The Deceiver, designed as a saltwater fly by Lefty Kreh, has become my favorite fall pattern for several reasons. It's reasonably durable (meaning you can catch two, maybe three pike on one before it's gnawed beyond repair). It's also easy to tie and sinks quickly. I usually fish Deceivers with sink-tip or full-sink lines. After casting, I allow the fly to sink to depth and then retrieve with a fast strip.

Although the version shown is basically a white fly, many other color combinations will take pike reliably, including yellow/red, black/yellow, and chartreuse/orange. I've slightly modified the original pattern by tying the wings in at the tail position in order to extend the length of the fly. You should experiment with colors and toppings.

I learned the value of the Deceiver during a fall trip to a favorite lake with some friends. We were casting Bunny Bugs. Fish we had. Follows we had. Hookups we had not. I had two white Deceivers in my vest, and on a whim, I tied one on. First cast, a fish. Second cast, another fish—and a fly shredded beyond repair. Deceiver number two was promptly tied on. One cast, a third fish. Second cast, a fourth fish—and a fly that might survive a cast or two to catch one more pike.

I looked up from the wounded fly to find myself surrounded by my companions, friends I had known for many years, all of whom were begging pathetically to be allowed to use my last Deceiver. And did I let my bosom buddies use that last battered Deceiver to catch a fish? Are you kidding?

## Materials for Lefty's Deceiver

| | |
|---|---|
| *Hook:* | Saltwater or salmon wet fly, e.g., Mustad #34007 or Tiemco TMC 811S, sizes 1 through 3/0 |
| *Thread:* | White and chartreuse |
| *Tail:* | White bucktail, shank length, inside white neck hackles (2 each side), extending 1½ times shank length |
| *Body:* | Silver tinsel |
| *Collar:* | White bucktail, extending nearly to tip of tail |
| *Topping:* | Chartreuse bucktail, as long as collar |
| *Throat:* | Several strands of red Krystal Flash |
| *Head:* | Chartreuse thread, lacquered |
| *Eyes:* | Applied with Faber-Castell Uni-Point Paint Markers |

Bunny Leech. *J. Berryman.*

## BUNNY LEECH

If you're not ready to upgrade to heavy tackle, but you still want a big fly that breathes and that casts fairly easily, the Bunny Leech is for you. The Bunny Leech also has a place in the vests of anglers who fish with heavy tackle. It's a fine choice when, for reasons best known to pike, the fish shy away from bigger, fatter Bunny Bugs. When this occurs, a switch to the slimmer Bunny Leech can save the day.

**Materials for the Bunny Leech**

| | |
|---|---|
| *Hook:* | Streamer, 3xl, or bass hook, e.g., Tiemco TMC 8089, size 2 |
| *Weight:* | Optional |
| *Weedguard:* | 25-pound hard mono |
| *Thread:* | White |
| *Tail/overbody:* | White rabbit strip, about 5″ long, tied in Zonker-style |
| *Body:* | Pearlescent Cactus Chenille, palmered with large white saddle hackle |
| *Head:* | White thread, lacquered |
| *Eyes:* | Applied with Faber-Castell Uni-Point Paint Markers |

## WHISTLER

This is another good light-tackle pike fly. In fact, it's even easier to cast than the Bunny Leech. The Whistler is also a good fly for open water because its ability to sink quickly makes it an effective fly for deep fish. The trade-off comes in the form of the Whistler's rather

Whistler. *J. Berryman.*

poor durability. Peacock herl and saddle hackles won't stand up to a pike's teeth, but because peacock herl is such a good fish-getter, I always carry some Whistlers and I recommend them to you.

## Materials for the Whistler

| | |
|---|---|
| *Hook:* | Saltwater or salmon wet fly, e.g., Mustad #34007 or Tiemco TMC 811S, size 2/0 |
| *Thread:* | Red |
| *Body:* | Black bucktail tied in at staggered positions along shank and extending 1½ shank lengths beyond hook |
| *Wings:* | Six black saddle hackles the same length |
| *Topping:* | Six to eight strands of peacock herl |
| *Collar:* | Red marabou, palmered one to two turns |
| *Eyes:* | Bead chain |
| *Head:* | Red thread |

## BLACK DIVING BUG

I include this fly and the other hair-bodied flies with some reservations. On the plus side, deer hair just can't be beaten for surface work; I've taken a lot of pike on deer hair flies. Deer hair is also quite light, and this particular pattern is especially suitable for use with lighter fly tackle. On the minus side, deer hair flies are more time consuming to tie and more expensive to buy than the average fly, and in an instant an angry pike can turn a lovely example of a fly tier's craft into something that resembles what Kitty coughed up last Wednesday.

As you probably know, divers are also very effective bass flies. When fishing waters that contain both pike and bass, divers in a variety of colors have a definite place in the flyfisherman's vest.

I fish divers two ways. With floating line, I retrieve them in a conventional manner, using short strips that cause the fly to dive. Then I pause and allow the fly to surface before I once again dive the fly. With sink-tip or sinking lines, I cast the fly, allow the line to sink, and then sink the diver with a "monster strip" or two. Then I have a choice. I can strip the fly in with relatively constant strips, which will keep it traveling at depth. More often, I pause and allow the diver to rise to or nearly to the surface. Then, more "monster strips" take it down into the depths again.

Particularly in the summer, the ability to work a column of water in this fashion and thereby determine where the pike are holding and feeding can be critical to your success.

Black Diving Bug. *J. Berryman.*

## Materials for the Black Diving Bug

*Hook:* Streamer, 3xl, or bass hook, e.g., Tiemco TMC 8089, size 2

*Weedguard:* 25 pound hard mono

*Thread:* Black

*Tail:* Black marabou extending one shank length beyond bend

*Wings:* Two grizzly saddle hackles, one tied on each side

*Topping:* Two to three strands of black Flashabou the same length as tail

*Head:* Spun and clipped deer hair with prominent collar two times the diameter of the head, with the hair behind the collar unclipped to extend over tail

## RABBIT STRIP DIVER

The Rabbit Strip Diver combines the virtues of the Bunny Bug with the enticing surface characteristics of a diver. Because of the rabbit-strip tail, it is significantly more durable than feather-tailed divers. Unfortunately, wet rabbit strip is a heavy material to cast, making the Rabbit Strip Diver best suited for heavier gear.

I use the same retrieves I use for the Black Diving Bug. As is the case with all divers, heart-stopping strikes can result when this fly is fished on the surface.

Rabbit Strip Diver. *J. Berryman.*

## Materials for the Rabbit Strip Diver

| | |
|---|---|
| *Hook:* | Saltwater or salmon wet fly, e.g., Mustad #34007 or Tiemco TMC 811S, size 3/0 |
| *Weedguard:* | 25-pound hard mono |
| *Thread:* | Black |
| *Tail:* | Black rabbit strip, 5″ long, topped with aqua marabou |
| *Head/collar/body:* | Black deer hair, spun and clipped to shape |
| *Eyes:* | 6mm plastic eyes |

## EDGEWATER SLIDER

The Edgewater Slider is my first choice for shallow water work on the surface. The foam is as tough as an old boot, as is the rabbit-strip tail, and pike can teethe on this fly for hours with no effect. Although the Slider is definitely heavier than a conventional diver, it's still a floating fly. When fishing this fly, I cast, pause for a time, and retrieve it with rapid, popper-style retrieves, essentially swimming the fly back to me. Be prepared to get wet, because when pike hit the Slider, water goes everywhere!

To attach the head, build up the thread underbody. Notch the front of the foam head to clear the weedguard attachment point at the eye. Apply slow-dry epoxy to the underbody. Install the foam head

Edgewater Slider. *J. Berryman.*

and slide it back so the weedguard can be tied in. Following attachment of the weedguard, slide the head forward to its final position.

## Materials for the Edgewater Slider

| | |
|---|---|
| *Hook:* | Saltwater or salmon wet fly, e.g., Mustad #34007 or Ticmco TMC 8118, size 2/0 |
| *Weedguard:* | 25-pound hard mono |
| *Thread:* | Black |
| *Tail:* | Black rabbit strip 4"–5" long, topped with six to eight strands of black Krystal Flash, topped with yellow marabou butt |
| *Wings:* | Yellow or black saddle hackle |
| *Collar:* | Black saddle hackle |
| *Head:* | Edgewater foam head |
| *Eyes:* | Doll's eyes |

## EDGEWATER WIGGLER

This is one of those flies that falls into the "wish-I'd-thought-of-that" category. The Wiggler resembles Flatfish and Lazy Ikes, which have been used effectively for pike for many, many years. The fly duplicates the motion of these plugs. With a rabbit-strip tail, the Edgewater Wiggler is probably more suited to casting with heavy

Edgewater Wiggler. *J. Berryman.*

tackle, but users of light tackle can tie on marabou or feather tails that will make the fly much easier to cast (but less durable).

I fish the fly with moderately paced, steady strips that produce a constant, enticing, wiggling action. Even though the fly has a large, floating head, the diving lip will take the Wiggler to depth quickly. If it seems to be running too deep, pause between strips. As is the case with all strip-pause retrieves, be prepared for a subtle take during the pause.

### Materials for the Edgewater Wiggler

(Note: To date, this fly is available only in a kit, in which the shaped foam body and hook are supplied.)

*Hook:*    Supplied in kit (size 2/0)
*Tail:*    Black rabbit strip, 4″ long, topped with chartreuse marabou
*Body:*    Black Cactus Chenille and palmered black saddle hackle (top and sides trimmed)
*Head:*    Foam Wiggler head from kit
*Eyes:*    Doll's eyes

### UMPQUA'S SWIMMING BAITFISH

I have good news and bad news. The good news is that I've caught more tigers on this fly than on any other, and when I leave the house on a tiger hunt, I *always* carry a half-dozen or so with me. Better yet, it is a comparatively light fly and can be cast well with light tackle.

The bad news is that, like all hair flies, it tends to be fragile. Worse yet, the Baitfish is a relatively difficult fly to tie, and seeing your careful handiwork torn to pieces by a tiger can be a real heartbreaker, depending, of course, on the size of the tiger that does the tearing.

This is one fly that I buy. Some folks enjoy the challenge of tying a difficult fly and don't mind when a fish tears the thing to pieces. If you fall into this category, by all means tie the fly yourself. Oddly, I have never fished the Baitfish as a floating fly. I always fish it with sinking line and use a strip-pause retrieve.

Umpqua's Swimming Baitfish. *J. Berryman.*

## Materials for the Umpqua's Swimming Baitfish

*Hook:*        Saltwater or salmon wet fly, e.g., Mustad #34007 or Tiemco TMC 811S, size 2/0
*Weedguard:*   25-pound hard mono
*Tail:*        Four white saddles 2 to 2½ times the shank length, inside of two blue dun saddles sided by two smaller white saddles
*Topping:*     Twelve strands of silver and peacock Krystal Flash
*Head/collar:* White and natural deer hair (white on bottom, natural on top), spun and clipped to shape
*Eyes:*        6mm plastic

## WOOLHEAD BAITFISH

This is a simple, durable fly that fits the same tactical niche as Umpqua's Swimming Baitfish. As with that fly, I fish the Woolhead with sinking line, but because it's not a floating fly, I bring the fly back with steady, swimming strips.

Because of the rabbit fur and wool construction of the Woolhead, it soaks up water like a sponge and may therefore be quite difficult to cast with light tackle.

Woolhead Baitfish. *J. Berryman.*

### Materials for the Woolhead Baitfish

*Hook:*      Streamer, 3xl, or bass hook, e.g., Tiemco TMC 8089, 1/0
*Weedguard:* 25-pound hard mono
*Thread:*    Gray
*Tail:*      Natural rabbit strip, topped with eight to ten strands of pearlescent Krystal Flash
*Collar:*    Natural rabbit strip, two wraps palmered forward
*Head:*      Ram's wool (not yarn), spun and clipped to shape
*Eyes:*      Doll's eyes

## EDGEWATER POPPER

There's a good chance there's something more fun than seeing a thirty-pound fish belt a popping bug, and when I find out what it is, I'll write a book about that, too.

Edgewater Popper. *J. Berryman.*

The problem is that pike turn cork bugs into sawdust and simply devour hair-bodied poppers. Although you may lose a tail feather or two (a defect that can often be repaired), Edgewater Foam Popping Heads will withstand the attacks of many pike. Foam poppers are also good choices for fishermen using light tackle.

When poppers are used for bass, many experts caution against making an excessive commotion with them. But when you use poppers for pike, pop them! As pike flies go, these poppers tend to run a bit small, and in order to convince a pike that there is a dinner-sized meal struggling on the surface, I think that healthy pops and chugs, followed by pauses, are in order.

## Materials for the Edgewater Popper

| | |
|---|---|
| *Hook:* | Saltwater or salmon wet fly, e.g., Mustad #34007 or Tiemco TMC 811S, size 2/0 |
| *Weedguard:* | 25-pound hard mono |
| *Thread:* | Yellow |
| *Tail:* | Four 4″ black saddles, inside two 4″ yellow saddles, topped with black marabou butt |
| *Collar:* | Yellow marabou saddle |
| *Head:* | Edgewater foam head |
| *Eyes:* | Doll's eyes |

## STUART'S SNOOKAROO

As its name suggests, this fly is primarily used for snook. It's also a very effective pike fly and, like Umpqua's Swimming Baitfish, is one that I don't tie.

With floating line, the Snookaroo is an excellent slider-type fly. With sinking line, it can be retrieved like the diver. Like all deer hair and feather flies, the Snookaroo is delicate for use with pike, but it has definite virtues due to its depth versatility and the fact that it can be cast effectively with light tackle. Tie this one if you like to tie.

### Materials for Stuart's Snookaroo

| | |
|---|---|
| *Hook:* | Saltwater or salmon wet fly, e.g., Mustad #34007 or Tiemco TMC 811S, size 2/0 |
| *Weedguard:* | 25-pound hard mono |
| *Tail:* | White bucktail twice the shank length, topped with strands of pearlescent Krystal Flash and red marabou, sided with grizzly hen hackles |
| *Collar:* | White deer hair, spun and clipped to shape, rear of hair left long to form collar |
| *Head:* | Black and white deer hair, spun and clipped to shape |
| *Eyes:* | 8mm plastic |

Stuart's Snookaroo. *J. Berryman.*

## BARR 'BOU FACE

My good friend John Barr invented this fly, and it is the fly of choice for light-tackle pike anglers who want a fly to duplicate the effectiveness of the heavy-as-lead Bunny Bug. It casts beautifully with six-weight gear and takes pike every bit as well as a Bunny Bug. The downside is that the marabou body is just not as durable as the rabbit-strip body of the Bunny Bug. But this is a great fly for beginning pike anglers who are making do with trout gear.

### Materials for the Barr 'Bou Face

*Hook:* Streamer, 3xl, or bass hook, e.g., Tiemco TMC 8089, size 2
*Thread:* Black
*Tail:* Black rabbit strip, topped with four to five strands of pearlescent Flashabou and four to five strands of black Krystal Flash
*Body:* Four black marabou plumes, distributed along the shank of the hook and tied in at the head
*Head:* Thread, to match body

Barr 'Bou Face. *J. Berryman.*

## D'S MINNOW

Darrel Sickmon is a fine fisherman, terrific teacher, innovative fly tier, and a good friend. Darrel started experimenting with Partridge of Redditch's Synthetic Living Fiber (SLF) dubbing about a year ago and managed to come up with incredibly lifelike imitations of just about every bait fish that swims. The flies are light, cast well, and sink without additional weight. They are durable enough to have a definite place in the pike flyfisherman's arsenal. My version shown here is rather plain, but Darrel mixes and blends various shades of SLF to produce imitations of baby bluegill, shiners, and shad that will make a pike drool.

## Materials for D's Minnow

| | |
|---|---|
| *Hook:* | Saltwater or salmon wet fly, e.g., Mustad #34007 or Tiemco TMC 811S, size 3/0 |
| *Thread:* | White |
| *Tail:* | White marabou threaded through pearlescent mylar woven tube |
| *Body:* | White SLF |
| *Gills:* | Red SLF |
| *Eyes:* | 6mm plastic, gold |
| *Head:* | Thread, coated with five-minute epoxy and sprinkled with fine glitter |

D's Minnow. *J. Berryman.*

Remember, not all the pike you'll catch will be twenty-pounders. *B. Snellgrove.*

# State-By-State Compendium of Pike Data

The information in this appendix comes from state game and fish officials across the country. It was compiled in 1992 and 1993. The depth of their responses to our queries, rather than the quality of the fishing in the individual states, determined the length and completeness of the report for each state. Some state agencies did not reply, and information for those states was taken from other sources. State records are listed under the name of each state. If no state record is listed for northern, muskie, or tiger, that fish is not present in the state or has just been stocked.

## Alabama
Muskie: 19 lbs., 8 oz. (1972)

Top State Pike Waters: Alabama's record pike was taken from the Wilson Dam tailwaters.

Spawn Dates and Temperatures: Muskies begin to spawn when water temperatures reach the mid-fifties.

Remarks: Although an occasional muskie may be found in Alabama, the state is not known as a prime pike fishery.

## Alaska
Northern: 38 lbs., 8 oz.

Top State Pike Waters: The Alaska Department of Fish and Game rates Minto Flats, George Lake, and all of the freshwater tributaries of the Yukon River (especially the lower portions) as prime pike waters. Generally, pike can be found in waters north of the Alaska range, including the North Slope, and in a few lakes in the Yakutat area. In addition, there are indications that fishermen have stocked pike in other state waters. The short Alaska growing season and cool average temperatures mean that pike will not grow as fast as their cousins to the south. For example, it takes from one to three years longer for Alaskan pike to reach sexual maturity. On the other hand, Alaskan pike also live about a third longer than other pike.

Stocking Program Details: Pike are not stocked in Alaska. All populations are natural and self-sustaining.

Spawn Dates and Temperatures: In Alaska, northern pike spawn from early May through early June, when water temperatures range from the mid-thirties to forty degrees.

Remarks: Alaska's Department of Fish and Game offers two publications of interest to the pike angler: *Northern Pike Sport Fisheries in Interior Alaska* and *Alaska's Wildlife: Recreational Fishing Guide*. Both can be obtained from the State of Alaska Department of Fish and Game, P.O. Box 25526, Juneau, Alaska 99802-5526.

## Arizona
Northern: 24 lbs., 3.0 oz., 47.5″

Top State Pike Waters: Lake Mary, Long Lake, and Stoneman Lake are, according to the Arizona Game and Fish Commission, probably the best pike lakes in the state.

Stocking Program Details: No state program for stocking any pike species exists.

Spawn Dates and Temperatures: In Arizona lakes, northerns spawn in March, when the water temperature reaches fifty degrees.

## Arkansas
Northern: 16 lbs., 1 oz. (1973)
Tiger: 13 lbs., 13 oz. (1985)

Top State Pike Waters: Arkansas is not known as a prime pike state. Portions of the Spring River and a few small lakes may hold pike. The state's record tiger was caught in Lake Ashbaugh, and the state's record northern was caught in Lake DeGray.

Spawn Dates and Temperatures: Northerns will begin spawning when water temperatures reach the low forties. Spawning success is thought to be low.

## California
Pike are not known to be present in California.

## Connecticut
Northern: 29 lbs. (1980)

Top State Pike Waters: Not known as an especially productive pike state, Connecticut anglers may have success in the Connecticut River and in 900-acre Bantam Lake. The state's record fish was caught in Lake Lillinonan.

Spawn Dates and Temperatures: Northerns begin spawning at ice-out. Their preferred spawning temperatures are between forty and fifty-two degrees.

## Colorado
Northern: 30 lbs., 1 oz., 48.5"
Tiger: 32 lbs., 9.5 oz., 48.5" (Quincy Resv., 1993)

Top State Pike Waters: The best Colorado northern pike fisheries are: Elevenmile Reservoir, Williams Fork Reservoir, Spinney Mountain Reservoir, the lower Yampa River, and Vallecito Reservoir. Tigers are also available in several Colorado lakes. Most recently, Quincy Reservoir in Aurora has been producing exceptionally fine fish, including the state record tiger.

Stocking Program Details: Northerns were stocked in Colorado many years ago. This program has since ceased, and northerns now maintain their populations via natural reproduction and the help of enlightened fishermen. Between eighty and 120 thousand six- to eight-inch tiger fingerlings are stocked each year.

Spawn Dates and Temperatures: Because of the extreme elevation differences in the state, Colorado northerns may spawn as early as March (on the plains) or as late as May (in mountain reservoirs). Temperature is the key. Look for Colorado northerns to spawn between thirty-five and forty-five degrees.

### Delaware

Pike are not known to be present in the state. Residents of Delaware are invited to make the short drive to Pennsylvania or other nearby states in their pursuit of pike.

### Florida

Pike are not known to be present in Florida.

### Georgia

Northern: 18 lbs., 2 oz. (1982)
Muskie: 38 lbs. (1957)

Top State Pike Waters: Georgia is not known as a prime pike state. The state's record northern was caught in Lake Rabun, while the record muskie came from Blue Ridge Lake.

### Hawaii

Pike are not known to be present in Hawaii.

### Idaho

Northern: 38 lbs., 9 oz. (Lake Coeur d'Alene)
Tiger: Recent introduction, nothing over 30″ reported to date.

Top State Pike Waters: Northerns were introduced illegally into Lake Coeur d'Alene and nearby lakes sometime in the 1960s, and the northerns have been naturally reproducing ever since. Northerns are also present in several other northern Idaho lakes, but Idaho Fish and Game Department officials indicate that Coeur d'Alene is the flagship pike lake. Stocking of tigers in ten Idaho lakes began in 1988, and the fish have only recently achieved the state's thirty-inch minimum length limit.

Stocking Program Details: Northern pike are not stocked in Idaho. The stocking of tigers is comparatively recent in Idaho, and it is not clear how well the hybrids will do in the state.

Northern: Idaho northerns spawn in April when water temperatures reach forty to fifty degrees.

### Illinois

Northern: 26 lbs., 15 oz. (1989)
Muskie: 28 lbs., 12 oz. (1989)
Tiger: 26 lbs., 2 oz. (1989)

Top State Pike Waters: The Mississippi River, as it flows through the northwest part of the state, offers some chance for trophy pike. Stillwater impoundments worth a look include: Fox Chain O' Lakes (northerns and muskies), Shabbona Lake, Lake Carleton, Lake George, and Clinton Lake. The state's record muskie was caught in Otter Lake. The record tiger came from Summerset Lake, and the state's record northern was caught in a "strip mine."

Spawn Dates and Temperatures: Northerns spawn from the middle through the end of March at water temperatures between forty-two and forty-eight degrees. Muskies spawn mid-April to early May when water temperatures range from fifty-four to fifty-eight degrees.

## Indiana
Northern: 26 lbs., 14 oz. (1983)
Muskie: 30 lbs. (1989)
Tiger: 22 lbs. (1988)

Top State Pike Waters: Consider Lake of the Woods, Lake Wawasee, and Brookville Reservoir. The state's record muskie came from the Whitewater River, while Indiana's record tiger was caught in Blue Lake. The state's record northern was taken from the Yellow River.

Spawn Dates and Temperatures: Northerns spawn from the middle through the end of March at water temperatures between forty-two and forty-eight degrees. Muskies spawn mid-April to early May when water temperatures range from fifty-four to fifty-eight degrees.

Stocking Program Details: An active tiger stocking program is carried out by the state.

## Iowa
Northern: 25 lbs., 5 oz., 45"
Muskie: 40 lbs., 5 oz., 50.5"
Tiger: 27 lbs., 2 oz., 47"

Top State Pike Waters: The Iowa Department of Natural Resources rates West Okoboji Lake and Spirit Lake as the best pike lakes in the state. Pools 9, 10, and 11 of the Upper Mississippi River are also rated highly. Iowa's muskie efforts are currently focusing on seven lakes, maintaining these populations by stocking about 7,000 eight-inch fingerlings annually. If all goes well, the state will eventually be able to provide a trophy-quality muskie fishery (rated by the state at a catch rate of 70 to 100 hours per fish). Survival rates of stocked muskies are unknown, but officials believe that there is a low survival rate among fish less than thirty inches in total length. Northerns are limited to the upper two-thirds of the state and are currently found in about fifty lakes and ten river systems. Although some populations are self-sustaining, many others are maintained through stocking. Nearly four million fry and 34,000 two-inch fingerlings are stocked annually. Fry are typically stocked in rearing ponds, marsh nursery areas, and most recently, in renovated lakes. Fingerlings are used in natural lakes where natural reproduction is insufficient to sustain a fishery but available habitat allows the fingerlings to grow rapidly. The annual harvest of pike by Iowa sportsman is considered to be low by state officials. Most Iowa pike are apparently caught by ice-fishermen.

Stocking Program Details: Fry are stocked in April, while fingerlings are stocked in May. Stocking rates vary from lake to lake; however, state guidelines call for northern fingerlings to be stocked in lakes over 100 acres with existing northern populations at a rate of five fingerlings per acre. Following winterkill, fry may be stocked at the rate of 1,000 fry per acre. It is against state policy to stock northerns in lakes containing muskies or tiger muskies. Fry are also stocked in streams at the rate of 1,000 fry per acre. In the case of tiger muskie, six- to seven-inch fingerlings are stocked in lakes over 100 acres in size. No more than five fingerlings per acre are stocked.

Spawn Dates and Temperatures: Northerns spawn in March and April, when water temperatures are between thirty-eight and forty-two degrees. Muskies spawn in April and May, when water temperatures range from forty-five to fifty degrees.

## Kansas
### Northern: 24 lbs., 12 oz (1971)

Top State Pike Waters: Kansas is not known as a top pike state. The state's record northern was caught in Council Grove Reservoir.

## Kentucky
### Northern: 9 lbs., 8 oz.
### Muskie: 43 lbs.
### Tiger: 13 lbs., 12 oz.

Top State Pike Waters: State Department of Fish and Wildlife officials point to Cave Run and Green lakes (stocking of muskies began in 1973 and 1977, respectively) as the state's prime lakes for muskies. Naturally reproducing populations of muskies are also present in the Licking and Green rivers. Other state muskie fisheries include Buckhorn Lake and the Barren, Kentucky, Little Sandy, and Red rivers.

Stocking Program Details: Roughly 14,000 nine- to thirteen-inch muskies are stocked annually in the state. Northerns and tigers are no longer stocked.

Spawn Dates and Temperatures: Northerns do not spawn successfully. Kentucky muskies spawn in April, when water temperatures reach sixty-five to sixty-eight degrees.

## Louisiana

Pike are not known to be present in Louisiana.

## Maine
### Northern: 26 lbs., 12 oz.
### Muskie: 22 lbs., 12 oz.

Top State Pike Waters: For muskie, state officials suggest Baker Lake. It is believed that muskies migrated into this Maine lake from Quebec after they were stocked there sometime in the early 1980s. This is now a self-sustaining population. For northerns, try Great Pond and North Pond. Northerns got their start in Great Pond after they were illegally stocked in the late 1970s. It is believed that some of these fish subsequently moved into North Pond. These populations have also become self-sustaining.

Stocking Program Details: Maine has no stocking program for fish other than salmonids.

Spawn Dates and Temperatures: Northerns spawn in late March and early April, when water temperatures range from thirty-five to forty-five degrees. Muskies spawn from late May to early June, when water temperatures reach fifty to fifty-nine degrees.

## Maryland
Northern: 23 lbs., 5 oz., 44.5″
Muskie: Not present (See text.)
Tiger: 26 lbs., 12 oz., 46″

Top State Pike Waters: The top pike water in the state is the Potomac River, including some of the river's tributaries and lakes fed by them. Most of this fishing will be for northerns and tigers, but state game officials indicate that there is some chance of muskies living in the Potomac. Department of Natural Resources personnel also rate the Youghighany River, Deep Creek Lake (on the Youghighany drainage), and Conococheague Creek (another Potomac tributary) as having the potential to produce good pike. In general, state game officials feel that most pike (tigers in particular) are caught accidentally by anglers pursuing other species.

Stocking Program Details: Both tigers and northerns are stocked. The tiger stocking program began in 1989. Approximately 2,000 "advanced" tiger fingerlings (eight- to ten-inch fish) are stocked annually from Paw Paw, West Virginia, to Edwards Ferry, Maryland, during the fall of the year. Conococheague Creek is also stocked. Some of the tigers currently resident in the Potomac have arrived from an unknown source.

According to state game officials, the following stocking activities have occurred in recent years:

1989: 20,000 1″ tigers into Conococheague Creek
1989: 5,000 4″-5″ tigers into Conococheague Creek
1989: 2,000 7″-8″ tigers into the Potomac River
1991: 13,000 1″ tigers into Conococheague Creek
1991: 1,500 7″-8″ tigers into the Potomac River
1991: 100 6″-8″ tigers into Little Pool
1992: 2,000 8″-10″ tigers into the Potomac River
1992: 8,400 5″-6″ northerns into Tridelphia Reservoir and Rocky Gorge

Spawn Dates and Temperatures: Maryland northerns spawn in March when water temperatures reach forty degrees.

## Massachusetts
Northern: 35 lbs., 47″
Tiger: 19 lbs., 4 oz., 40.5″

Top State Pike Waters: The only natural pike fishery in Massachusetts is the Connecticut River. The river and the oxbows and connected bodies of water associated with it always have the potential for good pike fishing, according to the Massachusetts Division of Fisheries and Wildlife. Other top state fisheries rely on stocked tigers and northerns. Rated as best in the state are: Charles River (northerns stocked in 1985 and 1989), Cochituate Lakes (131 and 195 acres, tigers stocked in 1980, 1981, and 1991; northerns stocked in 1985, 1987, and 1990), Onota Lake (617 acres, northerns stocked in 1987), Oxbow Pond (168 acres, tigers stocked in 1981), Pontoosuc Lake (467 acres, tigers stocked in 1980, 1981, 1986, 1989, 1990, and 1991), Quaboag Pond (531 acres, tigers stocked in 1982; northerns stocked in 1984, 1987, 1988, 1989, and 1990) and Quinsigamond Lake (475 acres, tigers stocked in 1981, 1983, and 1987; northerns stocked in 1984 and 1989).

Stocking Program Details: Tigers and northerns are stocked annually on a rotating basis. Between 7,000 and 12,000 six- to nine-inch fingerlings are stocked per lake.

Spawn Dates and Temperatures: Massachusetts northerns begin spawning at ice-out. Their preferred spawning temperatures are between forty and fifty-two degrees.

Remarks: State officials indicate that most of the pike fishing pressure in the state occurs during the winter season from ice-fishermen. They describe the pressure on pike during the warmer months as light, and indicate that most spring-through-fall pike are caught accidentally by bass fishermen.

## Michigan
Northern: 39 lbs., 51.5″
Muskie: 45 lbs., 51.5″ (northern muskellunge)
62 lbs., 8 oz., 59″ (Great Lakes muskellunge)
Tiger: 51 lbs., 3 oz., 54″

Top State Pike Waters: As is the case with Minnesota, there are far too many waters to list. At least fifty state impoundments have muskies or tigers occurring in them, while over sixty lakes have northerns.

Stocking Program Details: No pike species are regularly stocked in Michigan. Substantial natural populations are able to sustain themselves.

Spawn Dates and Temperatures: Northerns spawn from late March through early April when water temperatures average forty-five degrees. Muskies spawn throughout April when water temperatures average fifty degrees.

Remarks: Contact State of Michigan, Department of Natural Resources, Fisheries Division, P.O. Box 30028, Lansing, Michigan 48909-7258, to obtain a copy of *Select Fishing Waters for Certain Sport Fish.*

## Minnesota
Northern: 45 lbs., 12 oz.
Muskie: 54 lbs., 56″
Tiger: 33 lbs., 8 oz., 47″

Top State Pike Waters: There are literally hundreds of top-quality pike fisheries in Minnesota, and trying to list them here would be impossible. Even listing the "best of the best" would unavoidably eliminate some terrific fishing opportunities. For example, there are fifteen lakes in the metro-Minneapolis area alone that are stocked with tigers. We'd suggest you decide where you're going to be in Minnesota, and then contact the Minnesota Department of Natural Resources for additional details.

Stocking Program Details: Again, because of the sheer number of lakes involved, it's impossible to list the details of Minnesota's stocking program. Some lakes produce their populations of pike naturally, while others are stocked. In still other cases, DNR personnel have built artificial spawning areas for northerns.

Spawn Dates and Temperatures: Northerns spawn from March through April, when water temperatures reach thirty-nine degrees. Muskies spawn beginning in late April and continue through May. Their preferred water temperatures are fifty to fifty-five degrees.

Remarks: Contact the Minnesota Department of Natural Resources, 500 Lafayette Road, St. Paul, Minnesota 55155, (612) 296-6157. They can help you choose one or two lakes from among the ten-thousand-plus available options. My favorite? Basswood Lake in the Boundary Waters Canoe Area, but I haven't begun to explore the other available options.

## Mississippi
Pike are not known to be present in Mississippi.

## Missouri
Muskie: 41 lbs., 2 oz., 49.5" (Lake of the Ozarks, 1981)

Top State Pike Waters: Pomme de Terre Lake, Hazel Creek Lake, and Pony Express Lake.

Stocking Program Details: The state stocks only muskies, and the stocking program is limited to the lakes listed above. Northern and tiger stocking has been discontinued due to poor survival rates. Although muskies were stocked in Lake of the Ozarks, this program has been discontinued.

Spawn Dates and Temperatures: No evidence of successful spawning of northerns has been found. Spawning of muskies has been observed, but survival rates are poor.

## Montana
Northern: 37 lbs., 8 oz.
Tiger: 11.59 lbs.

Top State Pike Waters: Large northerns are taken from Timber and Fresno reservoirs in north central Montana, from Peck and Nelson reservoirs in northeastern Montana, and from Tongue Reservoir (state record northern) and a number of smaller reservoirs in the southeastern portion of the state. The Upper Flathead River and Nelson Reservoir are also worth a look.

Stocking Program Details: Northerns are most heavily stocked in Medicine Lake (150,000 fish, 1989), Lindsay Dam and Indian Creek Reservoir (200,000 fish each in 1990), Tongue River Reservoir (400,000 fish in 1991), and South Sandstone Reservoir (300,000 fish in 1991).

Spawn Dates and Temperatures: No dates or temperatures were given.

Remarks: The state offers the fine *Montana Fishing Guide*, free for the asking from Travel Montana, Department of Commerce (800) 541-1447. Although tigers are stocked in Montana, Montana Department of Fish, Wildlife, and Parks officials report difficulties with accessing tiger waters. Inquire at regional offices.

## Nebraska
Northern: 29 lbs., 12 oz. (1984)
Muskie: 35 lbs., 8 oz. (1990)
Tiger: 24 lbs., 4 oz. (1990)

Top State Pike Waters: The state's record northern was caught in Grove Lake. Lake McConaughy was the home of the state's record tiger, and the state's best muskie came from Merritt Reservoir.

## Nevada
Northern: 27 lbs.

Although not known as a pike fishery, there may be some pike in Basset Lake, near Ely. The state's record twenty-seven-pound northern was caught in Cumins Lake in 1978. Muskies and tigers are not known to be present in Nevada.

## New Mexico
Northern: 36 lbs.

Navajo Reservoir on the New Mexico–Colorado border may offer a trophy pike opportunity. Springer Lake and parts of the Rio Grande River may also hold pike. We suggest you inquire of state game officials before planning a trip, since the state is not known as a pike fishery. There is a tie for the state record pike between two thirty-six-pound northerns, one caught in Springer Lake in 1978, the other taken from Miami Lake in 1974.

## New Hampshire
Northern: 20 lbs., 9 oz.
Tiger: 11 lbs., 11 oz.

Top State Pike Waters: Not a top pike fishery, New Hampshire's record tiger came from the Connecticut River in 1982, and the 20 lb., 9 oz. record northern was caught from Spofford Lake in 1978.

## New Jersey
Northern: 30 lbs., 2 oz. (Spruce Run Reservoir, 1977)
Muskie: 38 lbs., 4 oz. (Delaware River, 1990)
Tiger: 29 lbs., (Delaware River, 1990)

Top State Pike Waters: The New Jersey Division of Fish, Game, and Wildlife lists the following lakes as the state's best northern fisheries: Spruce Run Reservoir (1,290 acres, northerns stocked since 1981), Budd Lake (376 acres, northerns stocked since 1981), Farrington Lake (290 acres, northerns stocked since 1987), Deal Lake (158 acres, northerns stocked since 1989), and Pompton Lake (204 acres, northerns stocked since 1989). In addition, muskies and tigers (apparently the result of natural hybridization) are present in the Delaware River.

Stocking Program Details: Four-and-a-half-inch fingerlings are stocked in June of each year. Roughly ten fish per acre are stocked.

Spawn Dates and Temperatures: Northerns spawn between March 15 and April 1 when water temperatures reach thirty-nine to fifty degrees. No data is available for muskies.

## New York
Northern: 46 lbs., 2 oz.
Muskie: 69 lbs., 15 oz., 64.5" (See "Remarks.")
Tiger: 35 lbs., 8 oz., 50"

Top State Pike Waters: For northerns, the New York State Department of Environmental Conservation suggests Lake Champlain (91,000 acres), Great Sacandaga Lake (22,000 acres), Tupper Lake (6,240 acres), Saratoga Lake (4,032 acres), Conesus Lake (3,420 acres), Cayuga Lake (42,956 acres), Seneca Lake (43,800 acres), Middle Saranac Lake (1,376 acres), and Lake George (28,000 acres). The St. Lawrence (97 miles), Raquette (18 miles), and Seneca (60 miles) Rivers are also considered to be very productive. For tigers and muskies, try Chautauqua Lake (13,376 acres, rated as the best in the state for muskie), Findley Lake (275 acres, has tigers), Waneta Lake (813 acres), Lake Durant (384 acres, a consistent tiger producer), Lime Lake (256 acres, tigers), Otisco Lake (2,200 acres, potential for trophy tiger), Cossayuna Lake (776 acres, tigers), or Canadarago Lake (2,000 acres, tigers). The St. Lawrence (97 miles, excellent fishery), Upper Niagara (30 miles, very good fishery, high catch rates), Mohawk (122 miles, tigers), Susquehanna (100 miles, tigers in localized concentrations), Allegheny (35 miles), and Great Chazy (19 miles) Rivers are also good muskie fisheries.

Stocking Program Details: Northerns are not stocked in New York; all populations are naturally sustaining. Muskies are stocked. In 1988, 157,000 muskies were stocked in forty-three New York State lakes. In 1989, 85,000 muskies went into thirty lakes; in 1990, 84,000 muskies were stocked in thirty-four lakes. In 1991, 78,000 muskies were stocked in thirty-three lakes. Tiger stocking began in New York in 1967. Between 1981 and 1987, between 113,000 and 150,000 tiger fingerlings were stocked in fifty-one lakes or rivers in the state.

Spawn Dates and Temperatures: Northerns spawn from late March to early May, when water temperatures are between forty and fifty-two degrees. Muskies begin spawning in late April and conclude by May. Preferred temperatures range from forty-nine to fifty-nine degrees.

Remarks: The state's record muskie was for many years considered to be the world record muskie. Recently, this fish has been disallowed by international record-keeping organizations. To date, it is still considered to be the New York State record muskie.

## North Carolina
Northern: 11 lbs., 13 oz.
Muskie: 38 lbs.
Tiger: 33 lbs., 8 oz.

Top State Pike Waters: State Wildlife Resources Commission officials report that best places to look for muskies include: the New River (stocked since 1978), French Broad River (stocked since 1970 to re-establish population), Nolichucky River (includes the Cane and Toe Rivers, stocked since 1977), Lake Alger (stocked since 1975), Fontana Lake, and the Tennessee River (stocking in these last two areas was discontinued in 1983, but some natural reproduction occurs).

Stocking Program Details: Northerns and tigers are no longer stocked in the state. Current stocking activities focus on the New river (250 fish stocked on even-numbered years), the French Broad River (1,300 fish stocked on odd-numbered years), and the Nolichucky River (175 fish stocked on even-numbered years).

Spawn Dates and Temperatures: State muskie populations appear to be spawning successfully, and although they certainly spawn in the spring, data on precise water temperatures is lacking.

Remarks: Two excellent documents covering state muskie populations are available: *Muskellunge Fishery Angler Diary Program* (1990) and *A Study of Riverine Muskellunge Populations and Habitate in North Carolina* (1985) from the Division of Boating and Inland Fisheries, North Carolina Wildlife Resources Commission, 37 New Cross North, Asheville, North Carolina 28095-9213. The 1985 paper, although technical in nature, is highly recommended for the pike angler seeking to learn more about river pike populations.

### North Dakota
Northern: 37 lbs., 8 oz. (Lake Sakakawea)
Muskie: 26 lbs., 5 oz. (Spiritwood Lake)
Tiger: 40 lbs., (Gravel Lake)

Top State Pike Waters: North Dakota Game and Fish Department consider Lake Sakakawea to be the crowning jewel of the state's pike waters. However, because of the state's generally cool temperatures, Sakakawea is certainly not the only resource available to pike anglers. Muskie are stocked in at least twenty North Dakota impoundments. As befits their greater popularity with local anglers, northerns are stocked in over 100 areas in the state.

Stocking Program Details: In 1991, about 250,000 northern fingerlings were stocked in 370,000 acre Lake Sakakawea. The state prefers to stock fingerlings rather than fry, and in 1991, stocking began in late May and continued through early June. In 1992, cool weather permitted excellent double-batching in rearing ponds, resulting in a statewide production of nearly five million northern fingerlings, nearly twice the usual yearly production.

Spawn Dates and Temperatures: Northerns spawn in April, when water temperatures are between forty and forty-five degrees. There is no evidence that muskies spawn in North Dakota waters.

Remarks: Northern fishing is the backbone of the North Dakota pike fishery. Muskie fishing is for trophy fish only and is held in high esteem by North Dakota fishermen. The North Dakota Game and Fish Department produces an excellent brochure, titled *North Dakota Fishing Waters*. You can obtain a copy by writing to: North Dakota Game and Fish Department, 100 North Bismarck Expressway, Bismarck, North Dakota 58501-5095.

## Ohio

Northern: 22 lbs., 6 oz., 43″ (Lyre Lake, 10/3/88)
Muskie: 55 lbs., 2 oz., 50.25″ (Piedmont Lake, 4/12/72)
Tiger: 26 lbs., 8 oz., 45″ (West Branch Reservoir, 8/25/84)

Top State Pike Waters: Over the past thirty years, the following locations have produced large muskies: Piedmont Lake, Pymatuning Lake, and West Branch Reservoir. Statewide, a yearly average of 941 muskies exceeding thirty inches in length were reported for the years 1985 through 1989. Ohio is working hard at improving muskie fishing opportunities throughout the state. For northerns, the picture is not so rosy. Past stockings of northerns have not produced significant fisheries, and stocking of northerns has now ceased. Limited northern fisheries based on natural reproduction exist in Lake Erie tributaries and a few other Ohio lakes.

Stocking Program Details: In 1990, 291,025 muskie fingerlings were released into ten state impoundments. In 1991, a total of 373,584 muskie fingerlings were released in ten locations in Ohio.

Spawn Dates and Temperatures: Northerns spawn from the middle through the end of March at water temperatures between forty-two and forty-eight degrees. Muskies spawn mid-April to early May when water temperatures range from fifty-four and fifty-eight degrees.

Remarks: From the stocking numbers indicated above, it's clear that Ohio is taking effective steps to provide quality pike angling for its residents. By contacting the Ohio Division of Wildlife, 952-A Lima Avenue, Findlay, Ohio 45840, you can obtain the following information: Ohio's Strategic Plan for improving muskie angling, copies of the state's *Husky Muskie Summary*, which details yearly muskie totals, stocking program details, and state record fish. You might also request a copy of *Muskellunge Fishing in Ohio*, a brochure produced by the Ohio Department of Natural Resources. The state also hosts an annual "Huskie Muskie" meeting and awards banquet. As you might expect, the state also has a very active Ohio Huskie Muskie Club. Contact Mr. Max L. Case, Jr. at 711 Ward Avenue, Girard, Ohio 44420.

## Oklahoma

Northern: 36 lbs., 8 oz. (Lake Carl Etling, 1976)

Top State Pike Waters: No specific information on top waters, spawning, or stocking programs was available for Oklahoma.

## Oregon

Pike are not officially present in Oregon, but limited pike fishing may be available in the eastern part of the state since both Washington and Idaho have pike.

## Pennsylvania
Northern: 33 lbs., 8 oz. (Allegheny Reservoir, 1980)
Muskie: 54 lbs., 3 oz. (Conneaut Lake, 1924)
Tiger: See "Remarks."

Top State Pike Waters: Although northern pike have been stocked across Pennsylvania, most of the better known fisheries are found in the Ohio River Basin and in particular the Allegheny River system. Pennsylvania is not noted for large northern pike. On the other hand, numerous waters offer the opportunity to take muskies of bragging size.

Stocking Program Details: A small northern stocking program exists, but most northern populations are naturally reproducing. The state does have a major stocking program for muskies and tigers. Although northwestern Pennsylvania is within the natural range of the muskie, natural reproduction has not been documented to any great extent. Some waters are stocked annually, while others are stocked on alternate years. In many Pennsylvania waters, both tigers and muskies are stocked. The theory is that while the tigers are easier to catch, muskies are longer lived and ultimately grow to a larger size. Generally, fingerlings are stocked from late summer to early fall. Between July 1991 and June 1992, the overall numbers of pike stocked in the state are as follows: northerns—1,600 fingerlings, split among two lakes; tigers—10,798 fingerlings, split among seventy-one locations in state lakes and rivers; muskies—76,921 fingerlings, split among fifty-five lakes and rivers.

Spawn Dates and Temperatures: Northern pike spawning activities often commence before ice-out on some lakes, as early as the first week of March. Some fish may still be ripe well into April. The state muskie population generally spawns during the first two weeks of April.

Remarks: For the purposes of state record keeping, tigers are lumped together with muskies. Based on reports from Area Fisheries Managers, some of the best places to take muskies are right at boat launch ramps. Often while setting out on an electrofishing trip, fish have been picked up within casting distance of the ramp or dock. Observers also report that muskies can often be found in deeper water than may generally be assumed by most anglers; a floating limb, tree or other accumulation of debris may provide shelter for muskies, even in open water. Pennsylvania Division of Fisheries Management personnel were exceptionally helpful in providing information for this entry. For additional information, contact Mr. Richard A. Snyder, Chief, Division of Fisheries Management, 450 Robinson Lane, Bellefonte, Pennsylvania 16823. An excellent summary of Pennsylvania pike fishing opportunities is contained in the October 1992 issue of *Pennsylvania Angler*. Officials can also provide a summary of the state's stocking program.

## Rhode Island
Rhode Island is not known as a pike fishing state. Some pike are said to be present in Worden Pond.

## South Carolina
Pike are not known to be present in South Carolina.

## South Dakota
Northern: 35 lbs.
Muskie: 40 lbs.
Tiger: 33 lbs.

Top State Pike Waters: Officials at South Dakota's Game, Fish, and Parks Department rate Oahe and Thompson lakes as the best stocked lakes in the state. Pike were introduced in those lakes in 1959 and 1988, respectively. Big Stone, Pickerel, Enemy Swim, and Clear lakes all offer naturally reproducing populations of northern.

Stocking Program Details: Northern pike are stocked only on a need basis, while tigers and muskies are stocked annually in specific waters according to a state master plan.

Spawn Dates and Temperatures: Northerns spawn in April when water temperatures reach forty-two to forty-eight degrees. Muskies generally spawn in May. No temperature data has been recorded.

## Tennessee
Northern: 20 lbs., 12 oz.
Muskie: 42 lbs., 8 oz.

Top State Pike Waters: Muskies can be found in Dale Hollow Lake (spawning population), Great Falls Lake (stocked population), Woods Lake (stocked population), and Plateau Streams Lake (stockers and a naturally spawning population). Northern pike are stocked in Melton Hill Lake.

Stocking Program Details: Muskies are regularly stocked; northerns are not. About 2,000 muskies are stocked each year, as many as half of which are stocked into streams.

Spawn Dates and Temperatures: Northern pike do not spawn successfully in Tennessee. The muskie population usually spawns in March at roughly fifty-two degrees.

## Texas
Northern: 18 lbs., 4.5 oz., 41″ (1981)
Tiger: 9 lbs., 1 oz., 32″ (1972)

Top State Pike Waters: None were listed.

Stocking Program Details: There is no stocking program for any pike species in Texas.

Spawn Dates and Temperatures: High water temperatures prevent successful spawning for northerns.

## Utah
Northern: 22 lbs., 44.5″
Tiger: Recently stocked

Top State Pike Waters: Redmond Reservoir (1,670 acres, northerns present since 1969) and Yubu Reservoir (11,000 acres, northerns moved in from Redmond Reservoir). Tigers have recently been introduced into Pineview Reservoir (stocked in 1991 and 1992).

Stocking Program Details: Only tigers are now stocked in Utah due to concern with naturally reproducing northerns adversely impacting populations of trout or endangered fish species. Information on spawning dates and temperatures was not available.

## Vermont
Northern: 30 lbs., 8 oz.
Muskie: 29 lbs., 8 oz.
Tiger: 17 lbs., 13 oz.

Top State Pike Waters: Lake Champlain has the potential to product trophy pike, as do several small lakes in the state. The state's record muskie was taken from the Missiquoi River in 1978. Vermont's best tiger was taken from the Connecticut River in 1987, and the champion northern came from Glen Lake in 1977.

## Virginia
Northern: 27 lbs., 12 oz.
Muskie: 45 lbs.

Top State Pike Waters: Although northerns are present in Virginia, Department of Game and Inland Fisheries officials report that no waters in Virginia could properly be considered a "top" water. Although the state did have a stocking program for tigers, the survival rates were poor. The muskie picture is quite a bit brighter. Virginia has stocked muskies in state waters for between fifteen and twenty years. State officials classify the Clinch, James, and New rivers as excellent muskie fisheries (particularly in the upper portions) and report that there are even some local guides specializing in muskies. Muskies are also stocked in several Virginia lakes. Burke Lake in northern Virginia and Retreat Lake in the southwestern portion of the state offer muskies for lake fishermen.

Stocking Program Details: Four- to six-inch muskies are regularly stocked in September. Statewide, between ten and fifteen thousand muskies are stocked annually.

Spawn Dates and Temperatures: High water temperatures prevent natural spawning for both northerns and muskies.

## Washington
Northern: 18 lbs., 6 oz.
Tiger: 7 lbs., 2 oz.

Top State Pike Waters: Not known as a prime pike fishery, Washington's record tiger came from Mayfield Lake in 1991. The 18 lb., 6 oz. record northern was taken from Long Lake in 1980.

## West Virginia
Northern: 22.06 lbs., 42.6"
Muskie: 43 lbs., 52.5"
Tiger: 28.13 lbs., 45"

Top State Pike Waters: West Virginia Division of Natural Resources rate Sleepy Creek, Warden Lakes, and the Ohio River as the best pike fisheries in the state.

Stocking Program Details: In 1991, 4,900 pike fingerlings were stocked into twelve West Virginia lakes and one river. In 1992, 3,000 fingerlings were stocked into thirteen lakes and one river.

Spawn Dates and Temperatures: Northerns spawn at the end of March when water temperatures reach forty-six degrees. Muskies spawn in early April when water temperatures rise into the low fifties.

## Wisconsin
Northern: 38 lbs. (9/15/40)
Muskie: 69 lbs., 11 oz. (10/20/49)
Tiger: 51 lbs., 3 oz. (7/16/19)

Top State Pike Waters: Wisconsin is blessed with many lakes and rivers that offer excellent fishing for both northerns and muskies. Muskies are common in the lakes and rivers of the headwater regions of the Chippewa, Flambeau, and Wisconsin rivers. In general, the best muskie fishing is found in the north-central portion of the state.

Northerns are more broadly distributed throughout the state, and excellent pike fishing can be found in the Mississippi and lower Wisconsin rivers. Fishing for trophy northerns is better in the state's larger, deeper lakes or rivers, because more abundant soft-finned prey is available.

Stocking Program Details: Northerns are not regularly stocked because state populations seem to be doing well with natural reproduction. The limited northern stocking that does occur is directed toward areas where spawning habitat has been lost due to the draining of wetlands, and overdevelopment of shorelines. Approximately 54,000 northerns and 150,000 muskie fingerlings are stocked each year in Wisconsin. The state's muskie stocking program is now over a half-century old. Most major state muskie waters are within the natural geographic range of the muskie, and although significant natural reproduction does occur, maintenance stocking is required to maintain population levels. Approximately 40,000 tigers are stocked each year in Wisconsin, but in relatively few areas.

Spawn Dates and Temperatures: Northerns spawn from late March through late April, when water temperatures range from thirty-four to forty degrees. Muskies begin spawning in mid-April and spawn through late May, when water temperatures range from fifty to sixty degrees.

Remarks: Wisconsin's tiger and muskie state records are also currently world records. See chapter 2 for more details. Write to the Wisconsin Department of Natural Resources, Bureau of Fisheries Management, P.O. Box 7921, Madison, Wisconsin 53707, to obtain their brochure entitled *Muskellunge and Northern Pike*.

## Wyoming
Northern: 23 lbs., 1 oz., 44⅜"
Tiger: 29.37 lbs., 49"

Top State Pike Waters: Northerns are available in only one lake in Wyoming, Keyhole Reservoir. The stocking of northern pike in the reservoir began in 1972. Wyoming's top tiger water is Grayrocks Reservoir. Initial stocking of tigers began in 1983.

Stocking Program Details: Although the Wyoming Game and Fish Department indicates that pike are regularly stocked in state waters, they do describe their stocking program as "variable."

Spawn Dates and Temperatures: No date or water temperature was available.

Remarks: For more details concerning Keyhole Reservoir, contact Bob McDowell, Area Fishing Supervisor, at (307) 672-7418. For information on Grayrocks Reservoir, contact Don Miller, Area Fishing Supervisor, at (307) 745-4046.

# INDEX